Table of Contents

All About Me!	3
Consonant Blends	4
Blends: fl, br, pl, sk, sn	5
Blends: bl, sl, cr, cl	6
Consonant Teams	7
Silent Letters	8
Short Vowels	9
Long Vowels	10
Vowel Teams	11
Y as a Vowel	12
Compound Words	13
Contractions	14
Syllables	15
Syllables	16
Suffixes	17
Prefixes	18
Reading for Details	19
Reading for Details	20
Following Directions	21
Sequencing: Yo-Yo Trick	22
Sequencing: A Visit to the Zoo	23
Same/Different: Venn Diagram	24
Same/Different: Cats and Tigers	25
Classifying	26
Classifying: Words	27
Comprehension: Types of Tops	28
Comprehension: Singing Whales	29

Copyright © 2006 School Specialty Publishing. Published by Brighter Child®, an imprint of School Specialty Publishing, a member of the School Specialty Family.

Printed in the United States of America. All rights reserved. Except as permitted under the United States Copyright Act, no part of this publication may be reproduced or distributed in any form or by any means, or stored in a database or retrieval system, without prior written permission from the publisher, unless otherwise indicated.

Send all inquiries to:
School Specialty Publishing
8720 Orion Place
Columbus, OH 43240-2111

ISBN 0-7696-7662-6

2 3 4 5 6 7 8 9 10 WAL 09 08 07

Predicting: Dog-Gone! 30
Predicting Outcome 31
Sequencing: ABC Order 32
Nouns 33
Subjects 34
Plurals 35
Verbs 36
Predicates 37
Subjects and Predicates 38
Adjectives 39
Adjectives 40
Sentences and Non-Sentences 41
Statements 42
Surprising Sentences 43
Commands 44
Questions 45
Counting 46
Counting: 2's, 5's, 10's 47
Patterns 48
Less Than, Greater Than 49
Ordinal Numbers 50
Addition 51
Addition: Commutative Property 52
Adding 3 or More Numbers 53
Subtraction 54
Place Value: Ones, Tens 55
2-Digit Addition 56
2-Digit Addition: Regrouping 57
2-Digit Subtraction 58
2-Digit Subtraction: Regrouping 59
Graphs 60
Fractions: Half, Third, Fourth 61
Fractions: Half, Third, Fourth 62
Geometry 63
Geometry 64
Measurement: Inches 65
Measurement: Inches 66
Time: Hour, Half-Hour 67
Time: Hour, Half-Hour 68
Money: Penny, Nickel, Dime 69
Money: Quarter 70
Answer Key 71–80

Name _____

All About Me!

Directions: Fill in the blanks to tell all about you!

Name _____
         (First)   (Last)

Address _____

City _____ State _____

Phone number _____

Age _____

Places I have visited: _____

_____

_____

_____

My favorite vacation: _____

_____

_____

_____

©2006 School Specialty Publishing   Basic Skills Helpers: Grade 2

Name _____

Consonant Blends

Consonant blends are two or three consonant letters in a word whose sounds combine, or blend. **Examples: br, fr, gr, pr, tr**

Directions: Look at each picture. Say its name. Write the blend you hear at the beginning of each word.

_____   _____   _____

_____   _____   _____

_____   _____   _____

_____   _____   _____

Basic Skills Helpers: Grade 2 ©2006 School Specialty Publishing

Name _____

Blends: fl, br, pl, sk, sn

Blends are two consonants put together to form a single sound.

Directions: Look at the pictures and say their names. Write the letters for the beginning sound in each word.

Name _____

Blends: bl, sl, cr, cl

Directions: Look at the pictures and say their names. Write the letters for the beginning sound in each word.

   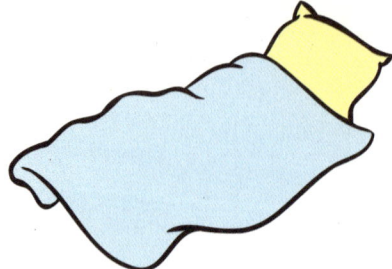   

_____ own   _____ anket   _____ ayon

   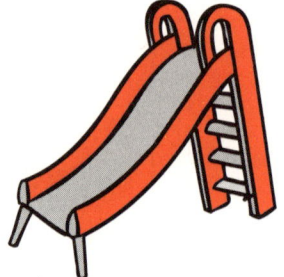   

_____ ock   _____ ide   _____ oud

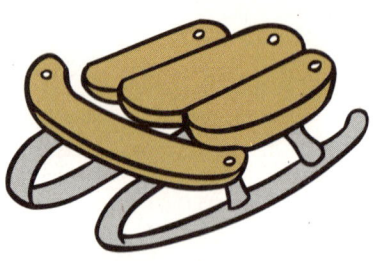      

_____ ed   _____ ab   _____ ocodile

Basic Skills Helpers: Grade 2   ©2006 School Specialty Publishing

Name _____

Short Vowels

Vowels can make **short** or **long** sounds. The short **a** sounds like the **a** in **cat**. The short **e** is like the **e** in **leg**. The short **i** sounds like the **i** in **pig**. The short **o** sounds like the **o** in **box**. The short **u** is like the **u** in **cup**.

Directions: Look at the pictures. Their names all have short vowel sounds. But the vowels are missing! Fill in the missing vowels in each word.

a   e   i   o   u

p__pp__t   h__mmer   p__pcorn   __l__ph__nt

t__l__v__sion   b__ttle   sh__v__l   th__mble

c__ndle   b__tt__n   p__nny   l__dder

©2006 School Specialty Publishing   Basic Skills Helpers: Grade 2

Name_____

Long Vowels

Long vowel sounds have the same sound as their names. When a **Super Silent e** comes at the end of a word, you can't hear it, but it changes the short vowel sound to a long vowel sound.

Example: rope, skate, bee, pie, cute

Directions: Say the name of the pictures. Listen for the long vowel sounds. Write the missing long vowel sound under each picture.

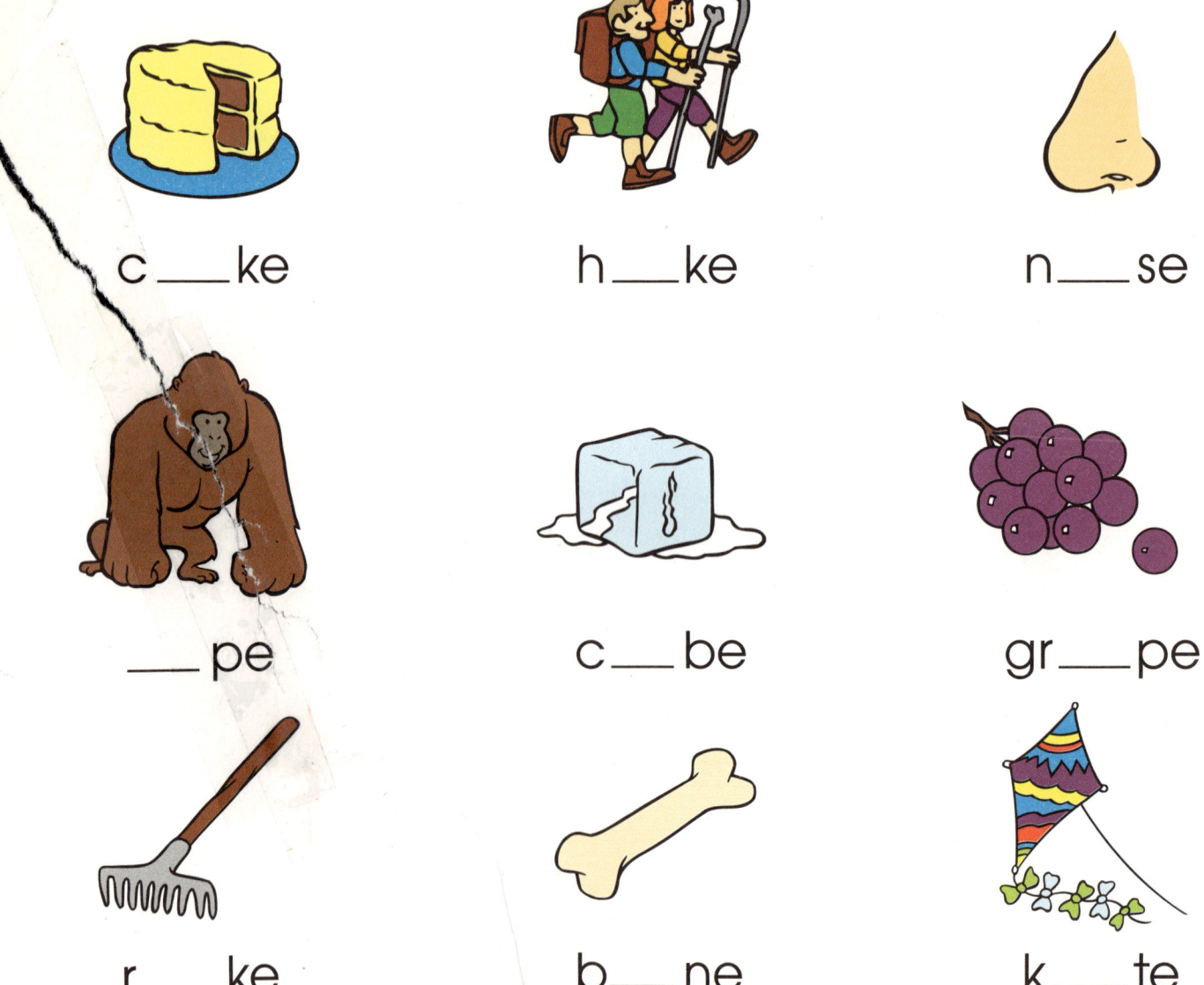

c___ke   h___ke   n___se

___pe   c___be   gr___pe

r___ke   b___ne   k___te

Basic Skills Helpers: Grade 2   10   ©2006 School Specialty Publishing

Name _____

Vowel Teams

The vowel team **ea** can have a short **e** sound like in **head**, or a long **e** sound like in **bead**. An **ea** followed by an **r** makes a sound like the one in **ear** or like the one in **heard**.

Directions: Read the story. Listen for the sound **ea** makes in the bold words.

Have you ever **read** a book or **heard** a story about a **bear**? You might have **learned** that bears sleep through the winter. Some bears may sleep the whole **season**. Sometimes they look almost **dead**! But they are very much alive. As the cold winter passes and the spring **weather** comes **near**, they wake up. After such a nice rest, they must be **ready** to **eat** a **really** big **meal**!

words with long **ea**	words with short **ea**	**ea** followed by **r**
_____	_____	_____
_____	_____	_____
_____	_____	_____
_____	_____	_____

Name _____

Y as a Vowel

When **y** comes at the end of a word, it is a vowel. When **y** is the only vowel at the end of a one-syllable word, it has the sound of a long **i** (like in **my**). When **y** is the only vowel at the end of a word with more than one syllable, it has the sound of a long **e** (like in **baby**).

Directions: Look at the words in the word box. If the word has the sound of a long **i**, write it under the word **my**. If the word has the sound of a long **e**, write it under the word **baby**. Write the word from the word box that answers each riddle.

| happy | penny | fry | try | sleepy | dry |
| bunny | why | windy | sky | party | fly |

my   **baby**

_____   _____
_____   _____
_____   _____
_____   _____
_____   _____
_____   _____

1. It takes five of these to make a nickel. _____
2. This is what you call a baby rabbit. _____
3. It is often blue and you can see it if you look up. _____
4. You might have one of these on your birthday. _____
5. It is the opposite of wet. _____
6. You might use this word to ask a question. _____

Basic Skills Helpers: Grade 2   ©2006 School Specialty Publishing

Name _____

Compound Words

Compound words are formed by putting together two smaller words.

Directions: Help the cook brew her stew. Mix words from the first column with words from the second column to make new words. Write your new words on the lines at the bottom.

grand	brows
snow	light
eye	stairs
down	string
rose	book
shoe	mother
note	ball
moon	bud

1. _____

2. _____

3. _____

4. _____

5. _____

6. _____

7. _____

8. _____

Name_____

Contractions

Contractions are a short way to write two words, such as **isn't**, **I've** and **weren't**. Example: **it is = it's**

Directions: Draw a line from each word pair to its contraction.

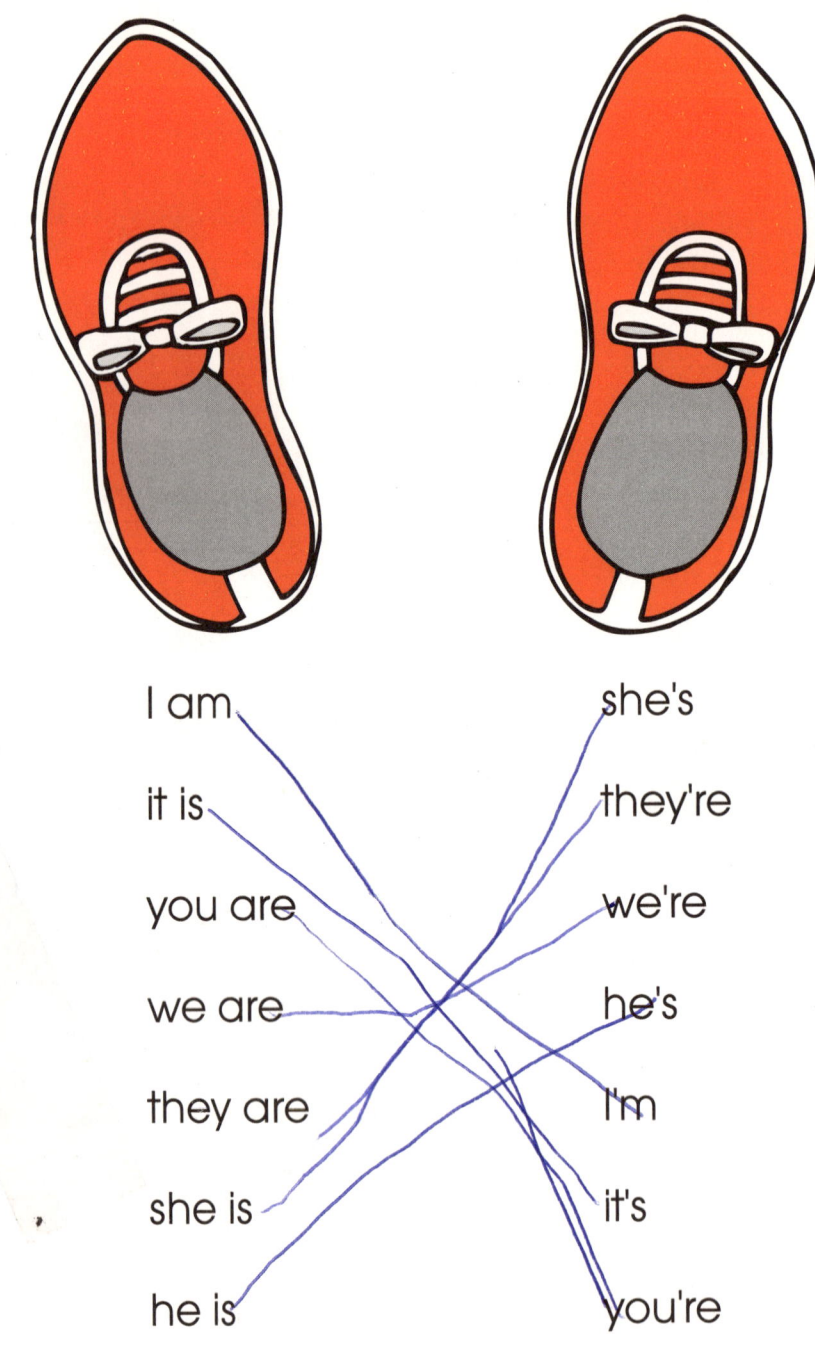

I am	she's
it is	they're
you are	we're
we are	he's
they are	I'm
she is	it's
he is	you're

Basic Skills Helpers: Grade 2   ©2006 School Specialty Publishing

Name _____

Syllables

Words are made up of parts called **syllables**. Each syllable has a vowel sound. One way to count syllables is to clap as you say the word.

Example: cat   1 clap   1 syllable
table   2 claps   2 syllables
butterfly   3 claps   3 syllables

Directions: "Clap out" the words below. Write how many syllables each word has.

movie ___2___   dog ___1___

piano ___3___   basket ___2___

tree ___1___   swimmer ___2___

bicycle ___3___   rainbow ___2___

sun ___1___   paper ___2___

cabinet ___3___   picture ___2___

football ___2___   run ___1___

television ___4___   enter ___2___

Name _____

Syllables

Dividing a word into syllables can help you read a new word. You also might divide syllables when you are writing if you run out of space on a line.
Many words contain two consonants that are next to each other. A word can usually be divided between the consonants.

Directions: Divide each word into two syllables. The first one is done for you.

kitten   kit   ten

lumber   _____

batter   _____

winter   _____

funny   _____

harder   _____

dirty   _____

sister   _____

little   _____

dinner   _____

Name _____

Suffixes

A **suffix** is a syllable that is added at the end of a word to change its meaning.

Directions: Add the suffixes to the root words to make new words. Use your new words to complete the sentences.

help + ful = _____

care + less = _____

build + er = _____

talk + ed = _____

love + ly = _____

loud + er = _____

1. My mother _____ to my teacher about my homework.

2. The radio was _____ than the television.

3. Sally is always _____ to her mother.

4. A _____ put a new garage on our house.

5. The flowers are _____ .

6. It is _____ to cross the street without looking both ways.

Name _____

Prefixes

Directions: Change the meaning of the sentences by adding the prefixes to the **bold** words.

The boy was **lucky** because he guessed the answer **correctly**.

The boy was (un) _____ because he guessed the

answer (in) _____ .

When Mary **behaved**, she felt **happy**.

When Mary (mis) _____ ,

she felt (un) _____ .

Mike wore his jacket **buttoned** because the dance was **formal**.

Mike wore his jacket (un) _____ because the dance

was (in) _____ .

Tim **understood** because he was **familiar** with the book.

Tim (mis) _____ because he was

(un) _____ with the book.

Basic Skills Helpers: Grade 2   18   ©2006 School Specialty Publishing

Name _____

Reading for Details

Directions: Read the story about baby animals. Answer the questions with words from the story.

Baby cats are called kittens. They love to play and drink lots of milk. A baby dog is a puppy. Puppies chew on old shoes. They run and bark. A lamb is a baby sheep. Lambs eat grass. A baby duck is called a duckling. Ducklings swim with their wide, webbed feet. Foals are baby horses. A foal can walk the day it is born! A baby goat is a kid. Some people call children kids, too!

1. A baby cat is called a _____.

2. A baby dog is a _____.

3. A _____ is a baby sheep.

4. _____ swim with their webbed feet.

5. A _____ can walk the day it is born.

6. A baby goat is a _____.

©2006 School Specialty Publishing   19   Basic Skills Helpers: Grade 2

Name_____

Reading for Details

Directions: Read the story about bike safety. Answer the questions below the story.

Mike has a red bike. He likes his bike. Mike wears a helmet. Mike wears knee pads and elbow pads. They keep him safe. Mike stops at signs. Mike looks both ways. Mike is safe on his bike.

1. What color is Mike's bike? _____

2. Which sentence in the story tells why Mike wears pads and a helmet? Write it here.

   _____

3. What else does Mike do to keep safe?

   He _____ at signs and _____ both ways.

Basic Skills Helpers: Grade 2   ©2006 School Specialty Publishing

Name _____

Following Directions

Directions: Read the story. Answer the questions. Try the recipe.

Cows Give Us Milk

    Cows live on a farm. The farmer milks the cow to get milk. Many things are made from milk. We make ice cream, sour cream, cottage cheese and butter from milk. Butter is fun to make! You can learn to make your own butter. First, you need cream. Put the cream in a jar and shake it. Then you need to pour off the liquid. Next, you put the butter in a bowl. Add a little salt and stir! Finally, spread it on crackers and eat!

1. What animal gives us milk? _____

2. What 4 things are made from milk?
 _____ _____ _____ _____

3. What did the story teach you to make? _____

4. Put the steps in order. Place 1, 2, 3, 4 by the sentence.

    _____ Spread the butter on crackers and eat!

    _____ Shake cream in a jar.

    _____ Start with cream.

    _____ Add salt to the butter.

©2006 School Specialty Publishing   Basic Skills Helpers: Grade 2

Name _____

Sequencing: Yo-Yo Trick

Directions: Read about the yo-yo trick.

Wind up the yo-yo string. Hold the yo-yo in your hand. Now, hold your palm up. Throw the yo-yo downward on the string. Hold your palm down. Now, swing the yo-yo forward. Make it "walk." This yo-yo trick is called "walk the dog."

Directions: Number the directions in order.

_____ Swing the yo-yo forward and make it "walk."

_____ Hold your palm up and drop the yo-yo.

_____ Turn your palm down as the yo-yo reaches the ground.

Name _____

Sequencing: A Visit to the Zoo

Directions: Read the story. Then follow the instructions.

One Saturday morning in May, Gloria and Anna went to the zoo. First, they bought tickets to get into the zoo. Second, they visited the Gorilla Garden and had fun watching the gorillas stare at them. Then they went to Tiger Town and watched the tigers as they slept in the sunshine. Fourth, they went to Hippo Haven and laughed at the hippos cooling off in their pool. Next, they visited Snake Station and learned about poisonous and nonpoisonous snakes. It was noon, and they were hungry, so they ate lunch at the Parrot Patio.

Write **first, second, third, fourth, fifth** and **sixth** to put the events in order.

_____ They went to Hippo Haven.

_____ Gloria and Anna bought zoo tickets.

_____ They watched the tigers sleep.

_____ They ate lunch at Parrot Patio.

_____ The gorillas stared at them.

_____ They learned about poisonous and nonpoisonous snakes.

Name _____

Same/Different: Venn Diagram

A **Venn diagram** is a diagram that shows how two things are the same and different.

Directions: Choose two outdoor sports. Then follow the instructions to complete the Venn diagram.

1. Write the first sport name under the first circle. Write some words that describe the sport. Write them in the first circle.

2. Write the second sport name under the second circle. Write some words that describe the sport. Write them in the circle.

3. Where the 2 circles overlap, write some words that describe both sports.

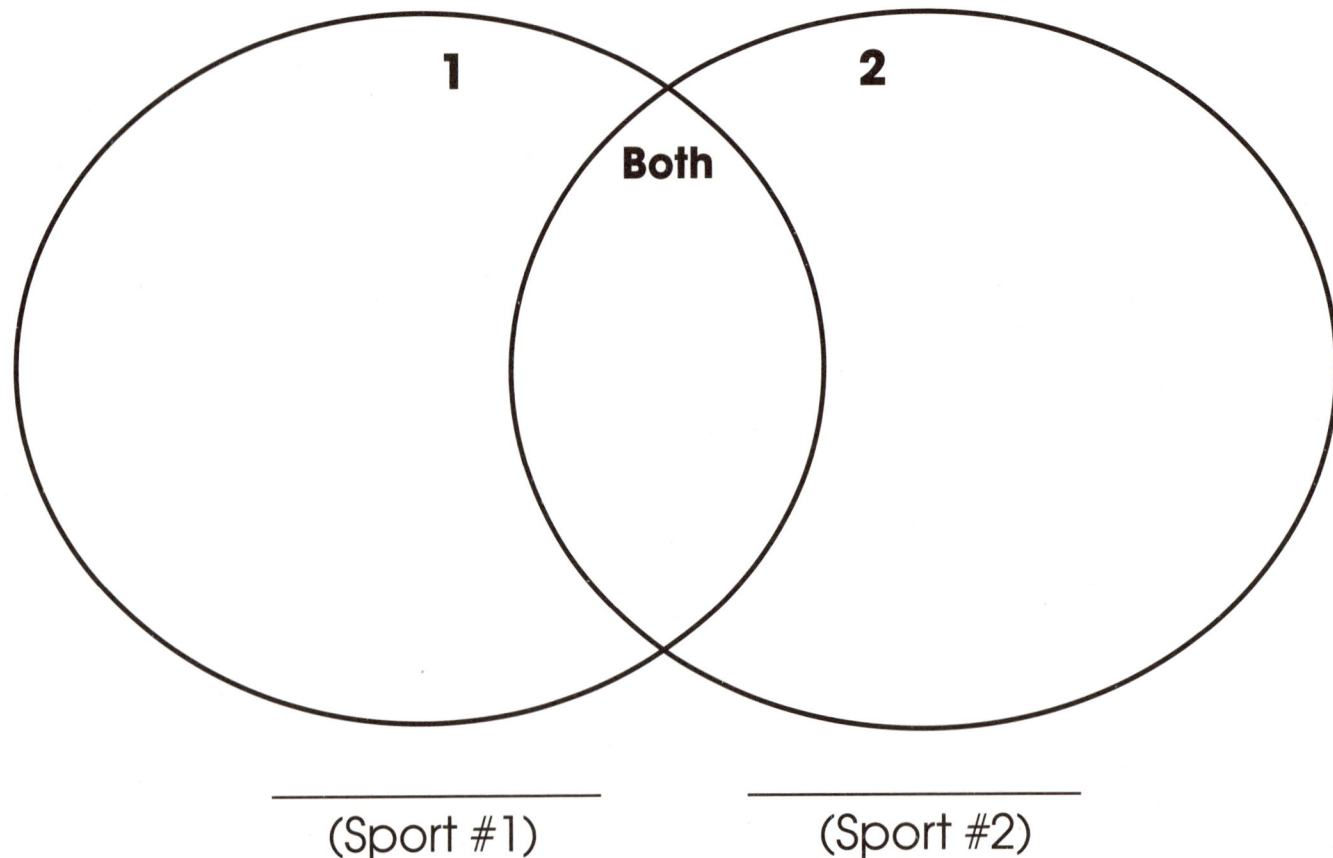

_____   _____
   (Sport #1)   (Sport #2)

Name _____

Same/Different: Cats and Tigers

Directions: Read about cats and tigers. Then complete the Venn diagram, telling how they are the same and different.

Tigers are a kind of cat. Pet cats and tigers both have fur. Pet cats are small and tame. Tigers are large and wild.

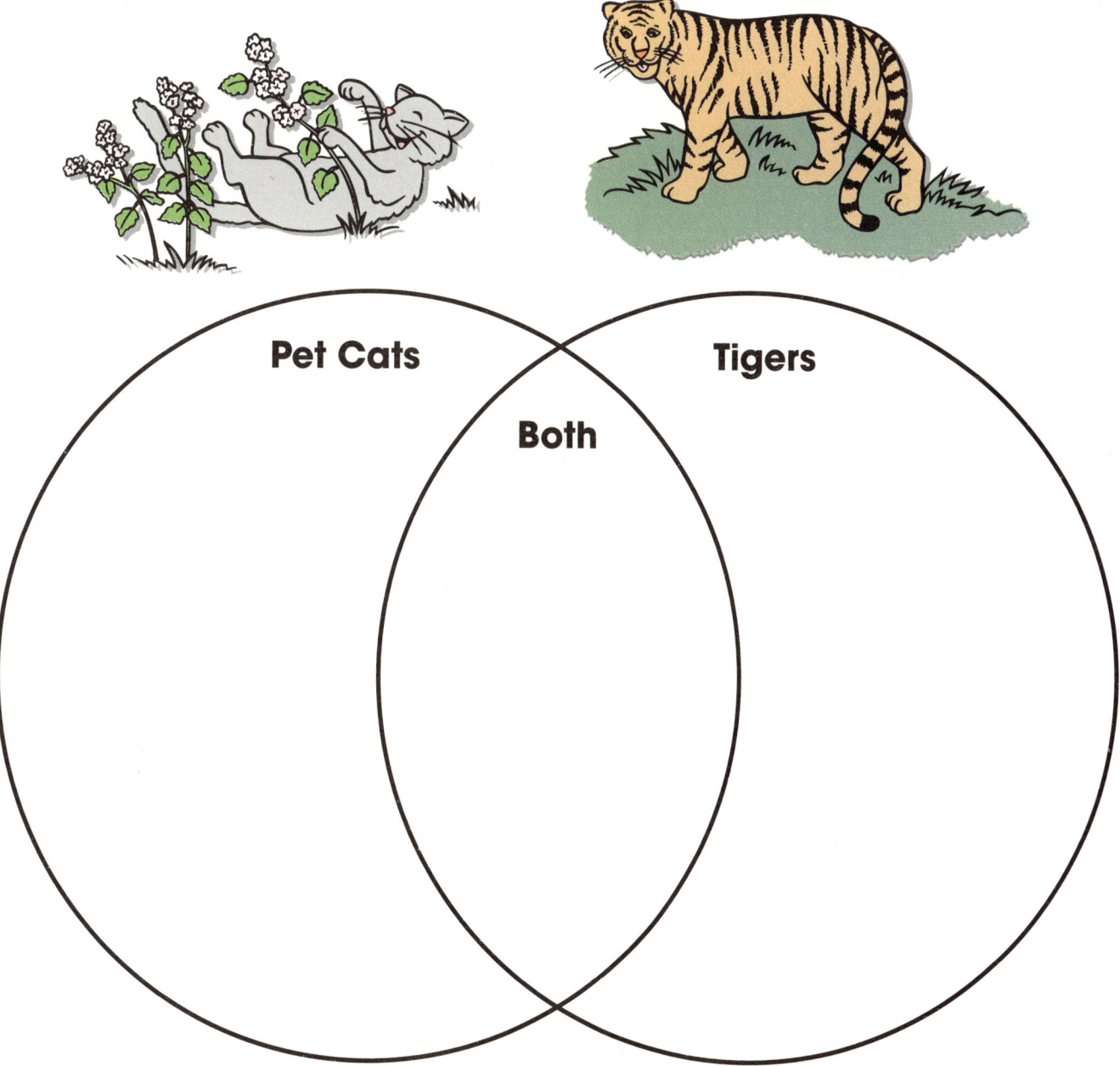

Classifying

Classifying is putting similar things into groups.
Directions: Write each word from the word box on the correct line.

baby	donkey	whale	family	fox
uncle	goose	grandfather	kangaroo	policeman

people   animals

 _____    _____

 _____    _____

 _____    _____

 _____    _____

 _____    _____

Name _____

Classifying: Words

Dapper Dog is going camping.

Directions: Draw an **X** on the word in each row that does not belong in that group.

1.	flashlight	candle	radio	fire
2.	shirt	pants	coat	bat
3.	cow	car	bus	train
4.	beans	hot dog	ball	bread
5.	gloves	hat	book	boots
6.	fork	butter	cup	plate
7.	book	ball	bat	milk
8.	dogs	bees	flies	ants

©2006 School Specialty Publishing   27   Basic Skills Helpers: Grade 2

Comprehension: Types of Tops

The **main idea** is the most important point or idea in a story.

Directions: Read about tops. Then answer the questions.

Tops come in all sizes. Some tops are made of wood. Some tops are made of tin. All tops do the same thing. They spin! Do you have a top?

1. Circle the main idea:

   There are many kinds of tops.

   Some tops are made of wood.

2. What are some tops made of? _____

3. What do all tops do? _____

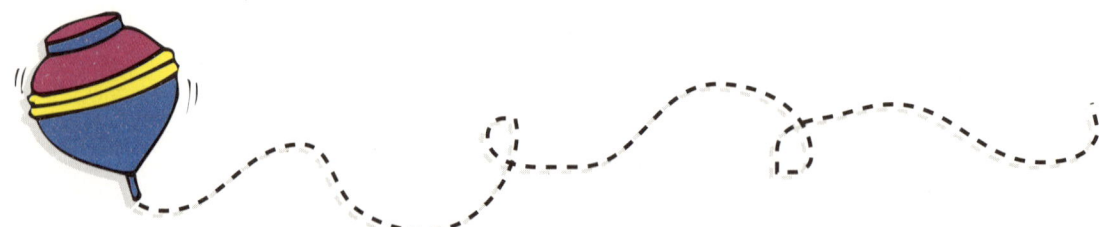

Name _____

Comprehension: Singing Whales

Directions: Read about singing whales. Then follow the instructions.

Some whales can sing! We cannot understand the words. But we can hear the tune of the humpback whale. Each season, humpback whales sing a different song.

1. Circle the main idea:

    All whales can sing.

    Some whales can sing.

2. Name the kind of whale that sings.

    _____

3. How many different songs does the humpback whale sing each year?

        1   2   3   4

©2006 School Specialty Publishing   Basic Skills Helpers: Grade 2

Name _____

Predicting: Dog-Gone!

Directions: Read the story. Then follow the instructions.

Scotty and Simone were washing their dog, Willis. His fur was wet. Their hands were wet. Willis did NOT like to be wet. Scotty dropped the soap. Simone picked it up and let go of Willis. Uh-oh!

1. Write what happened next.

_____

_____

_____

2. Draw what happened next.

Basic Skills Helpers: Grade 2   ©2006 School Specialty Publishing

Name_____

Predicting Outcome

Kelly and Gina always have fun at the fair.

Directions: Read the sentences.
Write what you think will happen next.

1. Kelly and Gina are riding the Ferris wheel. It stops when they are at the top.

   Kelly and Gina are not worried. They know the ferris wheel will be fixed.

2. As they walk into the animal barn, a little piglet runs towards them.

   Paint the Pig — Can I be Your Friend

3. Snow cones are their favorite way to cool off. The ones they bought are made from real snow.

   It was snowing.

4. They play a "toss the ring over the bottle" game, but when the ring goes around the bottle, it disappears.

   _____
   _____
   _____

Name _____

Sequencing: ABC Order

If the first letters of two words are the same, look at the second letters in both words. If the second letters are the same, look at the third letters.

Directions: Write 1, 2, 3 or 4 on the lines in each row to put the words in ABC order.

Example:

1. __1__ candy   __2__ carrot   __4__ duck   __3__ dance

2. _____ cold   _____ hot   _____ carry   _____ hit

3. _____ flash   _____ fan   _____ fun   _____ garden

4. _____ seat   _____ sun   _____ saw   _____ sit

5. _____ row   _____ ring   _____ rock   _____ run

6. _____ truck   _____ turn   _____ twin   _____ talk

7. _____ seven   _____ shoe   _____ soup   _____ smell

Basic Skills Helpers: Grade 2   ©2006 School Specialty Publishing

Nouns

A **noun** is the name of a person, place or thing.

Directions: Read the story and circle all the nouns. Then write the nouns next to the pictures below.

Our family likes to go to the park.

We play on the swings.

 We eat cake.

We drink lemonade.

We throw the ball to our dog.

Then we go home.

Name _____

Subjects

The **subject** of a sentence is the person, place or thing the sentence is about.

Directions: Underline the subject in each sentence.

Example: Mom read a book.
              (Think: Who is the sentence about? Mom)

1. The bird flew away.

2. The kite was high in the air.

3. The children played a game.

4. The books fell down.

5. The monkey climbed a tree.

Basic Skills Helpers: Grade 2   34   ©2006 School Specialty Publishing

Name _____

Plurals

Plurals are words that mean more than one. You usually add an **s** or **es** to the word. In some words ending in **y**, the **y** changes to an **i** before adding **es**. For example, **baby** changes to **babies**.

Directions: Look at the following lists of plural words. Write the word that means one next to it. The first one has been done for you.

foxes __**fox**_____   balls _____

bushes _____   candies_____

dresses _____   wishes _____

chairs _____   boxes _____

shoes _____   ladies _____

stories _____   bunnies_____

puppies_____   desks _____

matches_____   dishes _____

cars _____   pencils _____

glasses _____   trucks _____

©2006 School Specialty Publishing   35   Basic Skills Helpers: Grade 2

Name_____

Verbs

A **verb** is the action word in a sentence. Verbs tell what something does or that something exists.

Example: **Run**, **sleep** and **jump** are verbs.

Directions: Circle the verbs in the sentences below.

1. We play baseball everyday.

2. Susan pitches the ball very well.

3. Mike swings the bat harder than anyone.

4. Chris slides into home base.

5. Laura hit a home run.

Basic Skills Helpers: Grade 2 ©2006 School Specialty Publishing

Name _____

Predicates

The **predicate** is the part of the sentence that tells about the action.

Directions: Circle the predicate in each sentence.

Example: The boys ran on the playground.

(Think: The boys did what? )

1. The woman painted a picture.

2. The puppy chases his ball.

3. The students went to school.

4. Butterflies fly in the air.

5. The baby wants a drink.

©2006 School Specialty Publishing   Basic Skills Helpers: Grade 2

Name_____

Subjects and Predicates

The **subject** part of the sentence is the person, place or thing the sentence is about. The **predicate** is the part of the sentence that tells what the subject does.

Directions: Draw a line between the subject and the predicate. Underline the noun in the subject and circle the verb.

Example: The furry cat | ate food.

1. Mandi walks to school.

2. The bus drove the children.

3. The school bell rang very loudly.

4. The teacher spoke to the students.

5. The girls opened their books.

Basic Skills Helpers: Grade 2   38   ©2006 School Specialty Publishing

Name _____

Adjectives

Adjectives are words that tell more about a person, place or thing.

Examples: cold, fuzzy, dark

Directions: Circle the adjectives in the sentences.

1. The juicy apple is on the plate.

2. The furry dog is eating a bone.

3. It was a sunny day.

4. The kitten drinks warm milk.

5. The baby has a loud cry.

Name_____

Adjectives

Directions: Think of your own adjectives. Write a story about Fluffy the cat.

1. Fluffy is a _____ cat.

2. The color of his fur is _____ .

3. He likes to chew on my _____ shoes.

4. He likes to eat _____ cat food.

5. I like Fluffy because he is so _____.

Basic Skills Helpers: Grade 2 ©2006 School Specialty Publishing

Sentences and Non-Sentences

A **sentence** tells a complete idea. It has a noun and a verb. It begins with a capital letter and has punctuation at the end.

Directions: Circle the group of words if it is a sentence.

1. Grass is a green plant.

2. Mowing the lawn.

3. Grass grows in fields and lawns.

4. Tickle the feet.

5. Sheep, cows and horses eat grass.

6. We like to play in.

7. My sister likes to mow the lawn.

8. A picnic on the grass.

9. My dog likes to roll in the grass.

10. Plant flowers around.

Statements

Statements are sentences that tell us something. They begin with a capital letter and end with a period.

Directions: Write the sentences on the lines below. Begin each sentence with a capital letter and end it with a period.

1. we like to ride our bikes

_____

2. we go down the hill very fast

_____

3. we keep our bikes shiny and clean

_____

4. we know how to change the tires

_____

Name _____

Surprising Sentences

Surprising sentences tell a strong feeling and end with an exclamation point. A surprising sentence may be only one or two words showing fear, surprise or pain. **Example: Oh, no!**

Directions: Put a period at the end of the sentences that tell something. Put an exclamation point at the end of the sentences that tell a strong feeling. Put a question mark at the end of the sentences that ask a question.

1. The cheetah can run very fast

2. Wow

3. Look at that cheetah go

4. Can you run fast

5. Oh, my

6. You're faster than I am

7. Let's run together

8. We can run as fast as a cheetah

9. What fun

10. Do you think cheetahs get tired

Name _____

Commands

Commands tell someone to do something. **Example:** "Be careful."
It can also be written as "Be careful!" if it tells a strong feeling.

Directions: Put a period at the end of the command sentences. Use an exclamation point if the sentence tells a strong feeling. Write your own commands on the lines below.

1. Clean your room

2. Now

3. Be careful with your goldfish

4. Watch out

5. Be a little more careful

_____

_____

Name _____

Questions

Questions are sentences that ask something. They begin with a capital letter and end with a question mark.

Directions: Write the questions on the lines below. Begin each sentence with a capital letter and end it with a question mark.

1. will you be my friend

_____

2. what is your name

_____

3. are you eight years old

_____

4. do you like rainbows

_____

Name _____

Counting

Directions: Write the numbers that are:

next in order	one less	one greater
22, 23, ____, ____	____, 16	6, ____
674, ____, ____	____, 247	125, ____
227, ____, ____	____, 550	499, ____
199, ____, ____	____, 333	750, ____
329, ____, ____	____, 862	933, ____

Directions: Write the missing numbers.

13, 14, ___, ___, ___, ___

163, ___, ___, 166, ___, ___

821, ___, 823, ___, ___, ___

Name _____

Counting: 2's, 5's, 10's

Directions: Write the missing numbers.

Count by 2's:

2 4 ___ ___ ___

___ ___ ___ ___ 20

Count by 5's:

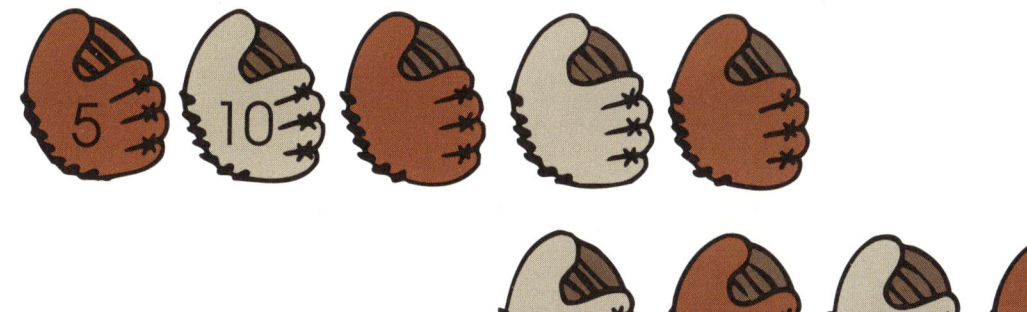

5 10 ___ ___ ___

___ ___ 40 ___ ___

Count by 10's:

10 ___ ___ ___ ___

___ ___ ___ ___ 100

Patterns

Directions: Write or draw what comes next in the pattern.

Example: 1, 2, 3, 4, __5__

1. 🔵 ⭐ ⭐🔵 ⭐🔵 🔵 ⭐ _____

2. A, 1, B, 2, C _____

3. 2, 4, 6, 8, _____

4. A, C, E, G, _____

5. 5, 10, 15, 20, _____

Name _____

Less Than, Greater Than

Directions: The open mouth points to the larger number. The small point goes to the smaller number. Draw the symbol < or > to the correct number.

Example: 5 > 3

This means that 5 is greater than 3, and 3 is less than 5.

12 ◯ 2   16 ◯ 6

16 ◯ 15   1 ◯ 2

7 ◯ 1   19 ◯ 5

9 ◯ 6   11 ◯ 13

©2006 School Specialty Publishing   Basic Skills Helpers: Grade 2

Name _____

Ordinal Numbers

Directions: Follow the instructions.

Draw glasses on the second one.

Put a hat on the fourth one.

Color blonde hair on the third one.

Draw a tie on the first one.

Draw ears on the fifth one.

Draw black hair on the seventh one.

Put a bow on the head of the sixth one.

Name _____

Addition

Addition is "putting together" or adding two or more numbers to find the sum.

Directions: Add.

Example:

```
  2
 +5
 ―――
  7
```

3	6	7	8	5	3
+4	+2	+1	+2	+4	+1

8	9	10	6	4	7
+2	+5	+3	+6	+9	+7

9	8	6	7	7	9
+3	+7	+5	+9	+6	+9

©2006 School Specialty Publishing 51 Basic Skills Helpers: Grade 2

Name _____

Addition: Commutative Property

The commutative property of addition states that even if the order of the numbers is changed in an addition sentence, the sum will stay the same.

Example: 2 + 3 = 5
3 + 2 = 5

Directions: Look at the addition sentences below. Complete the addition sentences by writing the missing numerals.

5 + 4 = 9   3 + 1 = 4   2 + 6 = 8
4 + __ = 9   1 + __ = 4   6 + __ = 8

6 + 1 = 7   4 + 3 = 7   1 + 9 = 10
1 + __ = 7   3 + __ = 7   9 + __ = 10

Now try these:

6 + 3 = 9   10 + 2 = 12   8 + 3 = 11
__ + __ = 9   __ + __ = 12   __ + __ = 11

Look at these sums. Can you think of two number sentences that would show the commutative property of addition?

__ + __ = 7   __ + __ = 11   __ + __ = 9

__ + __ = 7   __ + __ = 11   __ + __ = 9

Basic Skills Helpers: Grade 2   ©2006 School Specialty Publishing

Name _____

Adding 3 or More Numbers

Directions: Add all the numbers to find the sum. Draw pictures to help or break up the problem into two smaller problems.

Example:

```
  1 ○
  2 ○○
+ 3 ○○○
  6
```

```
  + 2 ⎱ 7
    5 ⎰
  + 2 ⎱ +6
    4 ⎰
      13
```

```
   3        8        3        8
   6        5        1        2
  +2       +4       +5       +9
```

```
   2        3        4        6
   8        6        1        7
   4        5        2        3
  +3       +2       +5       +1
```

53

Subtraction

Subtraction is "taking away" or subtracting one number from another to find the difference.

Directions: Subtract.

Example:

$$\begin{array}{r} 4 \\ -3 \\ \hline 1 \end{array}$$

$$\begin{array}{r} 5 \\ -3 \\ \hline \end{array} \quad \begin{array}{r} 6 \\ -1 \\ \hline \end{array} \quad \begin{array}{r} 4 \\ -3 \\ \hline \end{array} \quad \begin{array}{r} 3 \\ -1 \\ \hline \end{array} \quad \begin{array}{r} 2 \\ -0 \\ \hline \end{array} \quad \begin{array}{r} 1 \\ -1 \\ \hline \end{array}$$

$$\begin{array}{r} 9 \\ -2 \\ \hline \end{array} \quad \begin{array}{r} 7 \\ -4 \\ \hline \end{array} \quad \begin{array}{r} 10 \\ -5 \\ \hline \end{array} \quad \begin{array}{r} 14 \\ -6 \\ \hline \end{array} \quad \begin{array}{r} 15 \\ -9 \\ \hline \end{array} \quad \begin{array}{r} 12 \\ -3 \\ \hline \end{array}$$

$$\begin{array}{r} 18 \\ -8 \\ \hline \end{array} \quad \begin{array}{r} 13 \\ -5 \\ \hline \end{array} \quad \begin{array}{r} 14 \\ -7 \\ \hline \end{array} \quad \begin{array}{r} 11 \\ -4 \\ \hline \end{array} \quad \begin{array}{r} 17 \\ -9 \\ \hline \end{array} \quad \begin{array}{r} 16 \\ -8 \\ \hline \end{array}$$

Basic Skills Helpers: Grade 2

Name _____

2-Digit Addition: Regrouping

Addition is "putting together" or adding two or more numbers to find the sum. Regrouping is using **ten ones** to form **one ten, ten tens** to form **one 100, fifteen ones** to form **one ten** and **five ones** and so on.

Directions: Study the examples. Follow the steps to add.

Example:
```
  14
+  8
```

Step 1: Add the ones.

tens	ones
1	4
+	8
	12

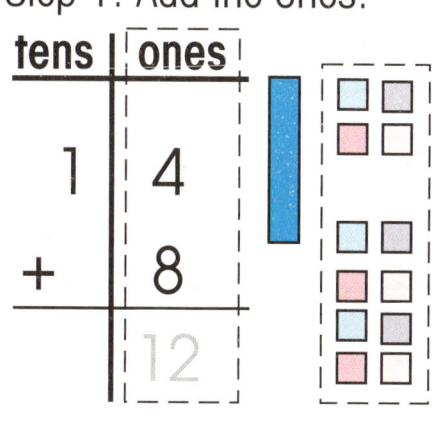

Step 2: Regroup the tens.

tens	ones
1	
1	4
+	8
	2

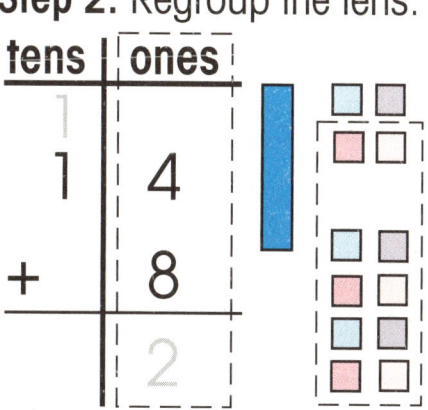

Step 3: Add the tens.

tens	ones
1	
1	4
+	8
2	2

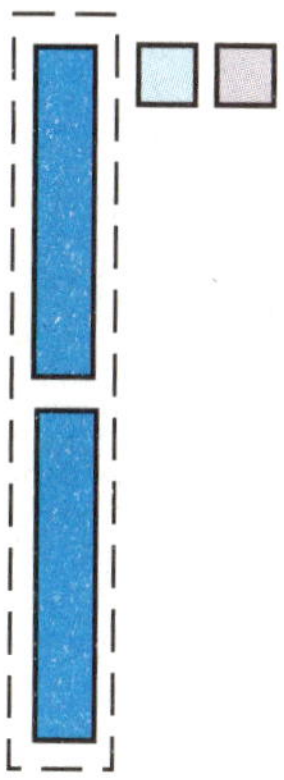

tens	ones
1	
1	6
+3	7
5	3

tens	ones
1	
3	8
+5	3
9	1

tens	ones
1	
2	4
+4	7
7	1

```
 28    32    54    19    44    25    29    79
+17   +38   +25   +55   +48   +64   +33   +15
```

©2006 School Specialty Publishing   57   Basic Skills Helpers: Grade 2

Name _____

2-Digit Subtraction

Directions: Study the example. Follow the steps to subtract.

Example:
$$\begin{array}{r}28\\-14\end{array}$$

Step 1: Subtract the ones.

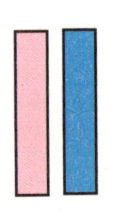

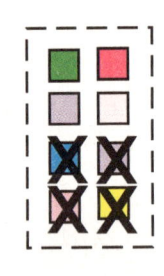

Step 2: Subtract the tens.

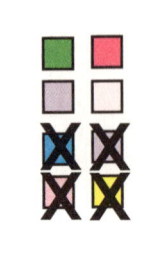

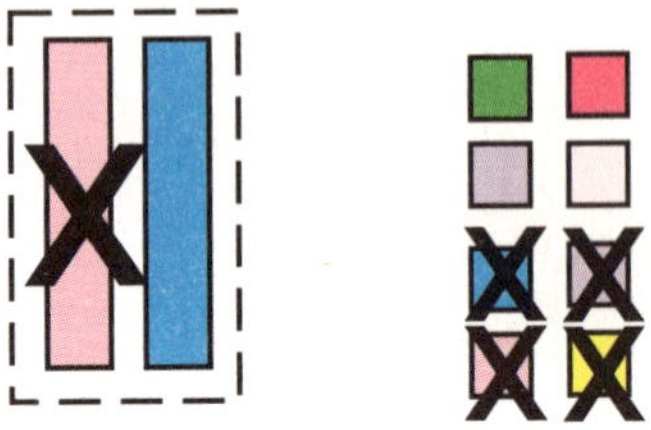

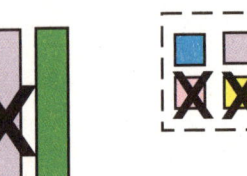

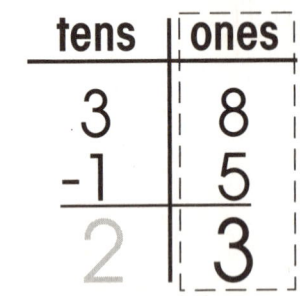

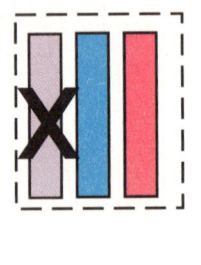

24	61	77	85	57	87	59	96
−12	−30	−44	−24	−23	−33	−34	−16

29	74	46	69	95	33	78	22
−15	−51	−32	−35	−32	−33	−26	−11

Basic Skills Helpers: Grade 2 ©2006 School Specialty Publishing

Name _____

2-Digit Subtraction: Regrouping

Subtraction is "taking away" or subtracting one number from another to find the difference. Regrouping is using **one ten to form ten ones, one 100 to form ten tens** and so on.

Directions: Study the examples. Follow the steps to subtract.

Example: 37
              −19

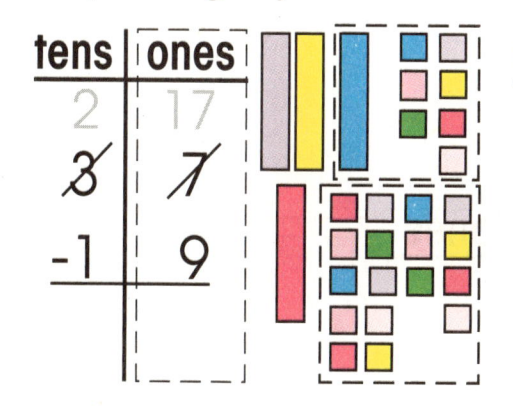

Step 1: Regroup.   **Step 2:** Subtract the ones.   **Step 3:** Subtract the tens.

tens	ones
2	17
3̸	7̸
−1	9

tens	ones
2	17
3̸	7̸
−1	9
	8

tens	ones
2	17
3̸	7̸
−1	9
1	8

tens	ones
0	12
1̸	2̸
−	9
	3

tens	ones
2	14
3̸	4̸
−1	6
1	8

tens	ones
3	15
4̸	5̸
−2	9
1	6

```
 28      46      12      30      52      47      21      45
−19     −18     − 8     −12     −25     −35     −13     −25
```

©2006 School Specialty Publishing   59   Basic Skills Helpers: Grade 2

Name _____

Graphs

A graph is a drawing that shows information about numbers.

Directions: Count the apples in each row. Color the boxes to show how many apples have bites taken out of them.

Example:

| 1 | 2 | 3 | 4 | 5 | 6 | 7 | 8 |

Basic Skills Helpers: Grade 2   60   ©2006 School Specialty Publishing

Name_____

Fractions: Half, Third, Fourth

A fraction is a number that names part of a whole, such as $\frac{1}{2}$ or $\frac{1}{3}$.

Directions: Study the examples. Color the correct fraction of each shape.

Examples:

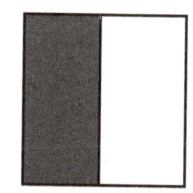

shaded part   1
equal parts   2
$\frac{1}{2}$ (one-half) shaded

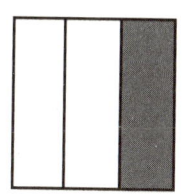

shaded part   1
equal parts   3
$\frac{1}{3}$ (one-third) shaded

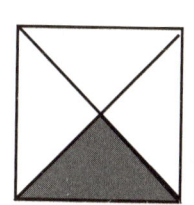

shaded part   1
equal parts   4
$\frac{1}{4}$ (one-fourth) shaded

Color: $\frac{1}{3}$ red

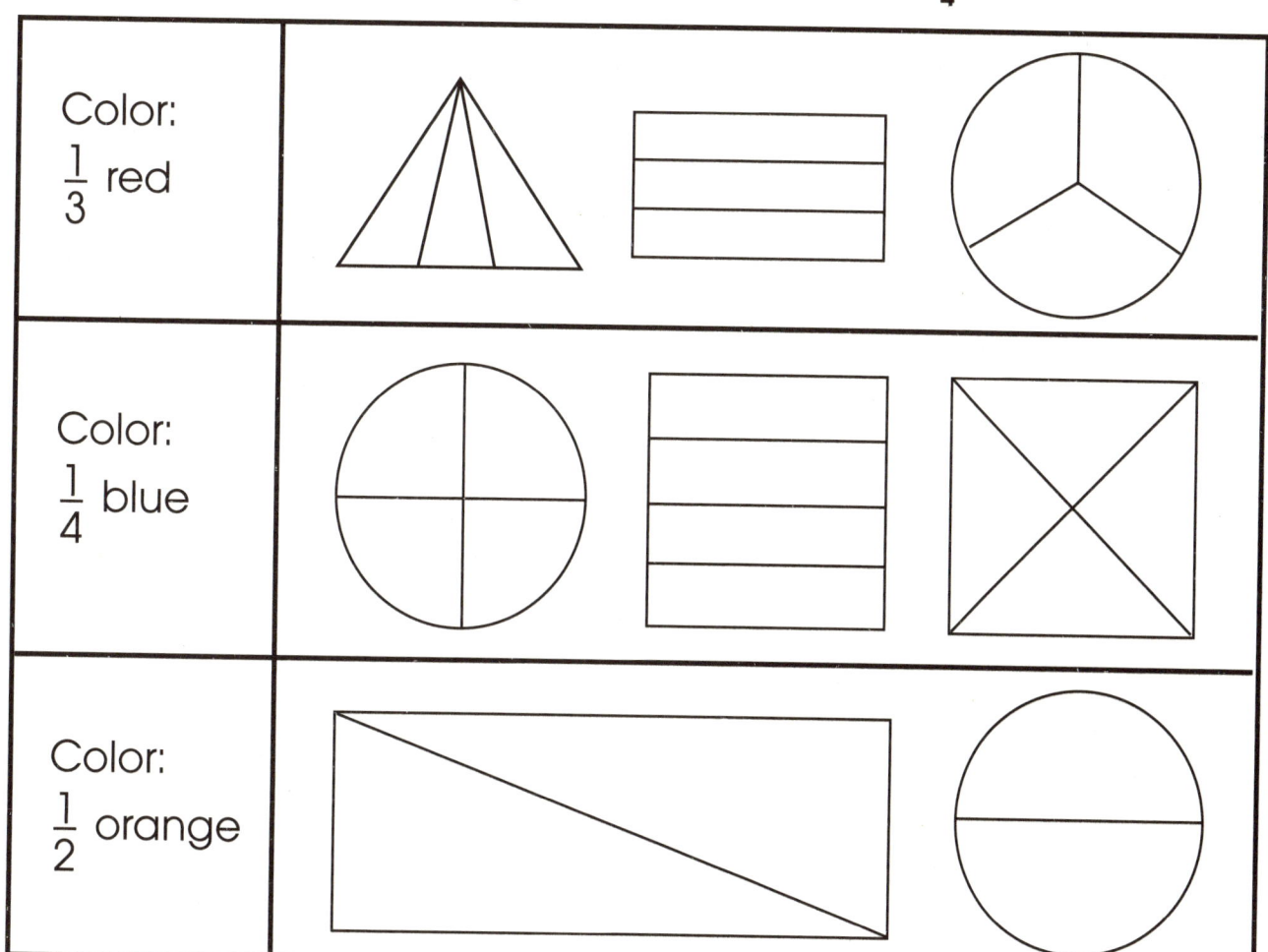

Color: $\frac{1}{4}$ blue

Color: $\frac{1}{2}$ orange

©2006 School Specialty Publishing

Basic Skills Helpers: Grade 2

Name_____

Fractions: Half, Third, Fourth

Directions: Draw a line from the fraction to the correct shape.

$\frac{1}{4}$ shaded

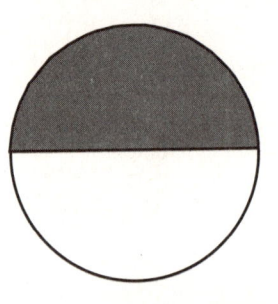

$\frac{2}{4}$ shaded

$\frac{1}{2}$ shaded

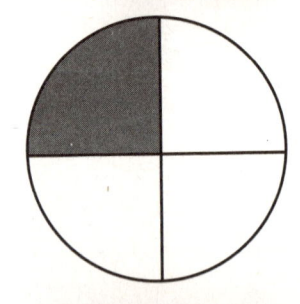

$\frac{1}{3}$ shaded

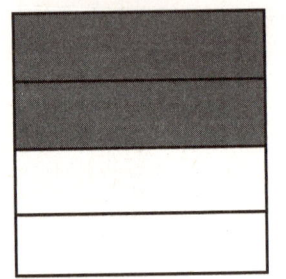

$\frac{2}{3}$ shaded

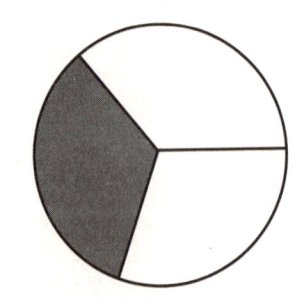

Name_____

Geometry

Geometry is mathematics that has to do with lines and shapes.

Directions: Color the shapes.

Color the triangles blue.
Color the circles red.
Color the squares green.
Color the rectangles pink.

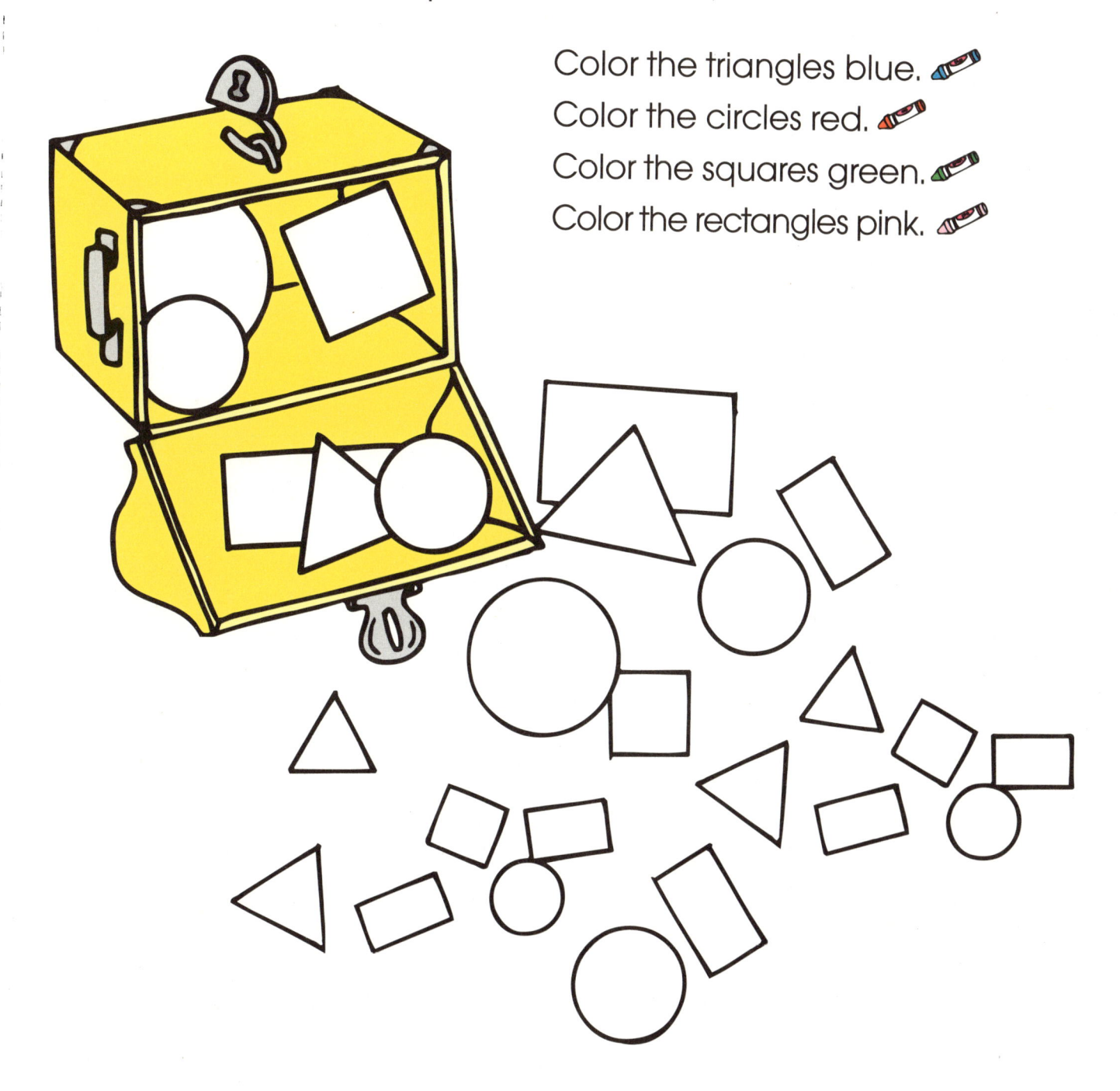

Name _____

Geometry

Directions: Draw a line from the word to the shape.

Use a red line for circles.   Use a yellow line for rectangles.
Use a blue line for squares.   Use a green line for triangles.

Circle   **Square**   **Triangle**   **Rectangle**

Basic Skills Helpers: Grade 2   64   ©2006 School Specialty Publishing

Name _____

Measurement: Inches

Directions: Cut out the ruler. Measure each object to the nearest inch.

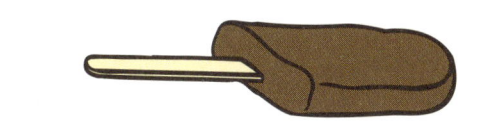

_____ inches

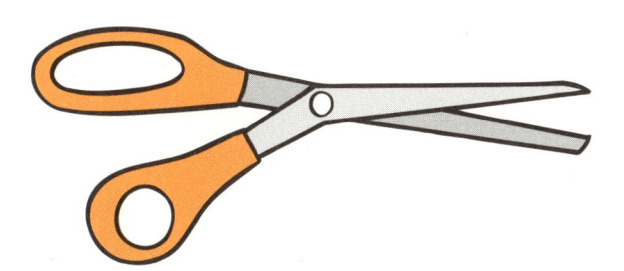

_____ inches

_____ inches

Measurement

Directions: Measure objects around your house. Write the measurement to the nearest inch.

can of soup   _____ inches

pen   _____ inches

toothbrush   _____ inches

paper clip   _____ inches

small toy   _____ inches

©2006 School Specialty Publishing   65   Basic Skills Helpers: Grade 2

Page is blank for cutting exercise on previous page.

Time: Hour, Half-Hour

An hour is sixty minutes. The short hand of a clock tells the hour. It is written **0:00**, such as **5:00**. A half-hour is thirty minutes. When the long hand of the clock is pointing to the six, the time is on the half-hour. It is written **:30**, such as **5:30**.

Directions: Study the examples. Tell what time it is on each clock.

Examples:

9:00

The minute hand is on the 12.
The hour hand is on the 9.
It is 9 o'clock.

4:30

The minute hand is on the 6.
The hour hand is *between* the 4 and 5.
It is 4:30.

©2006 School Specialty Publishing   67   Basic Skills Helpers: Grade 2

Name _____

Time: Hour, Half-Hour

Directions: Draw lines between the clocks that show the same time.

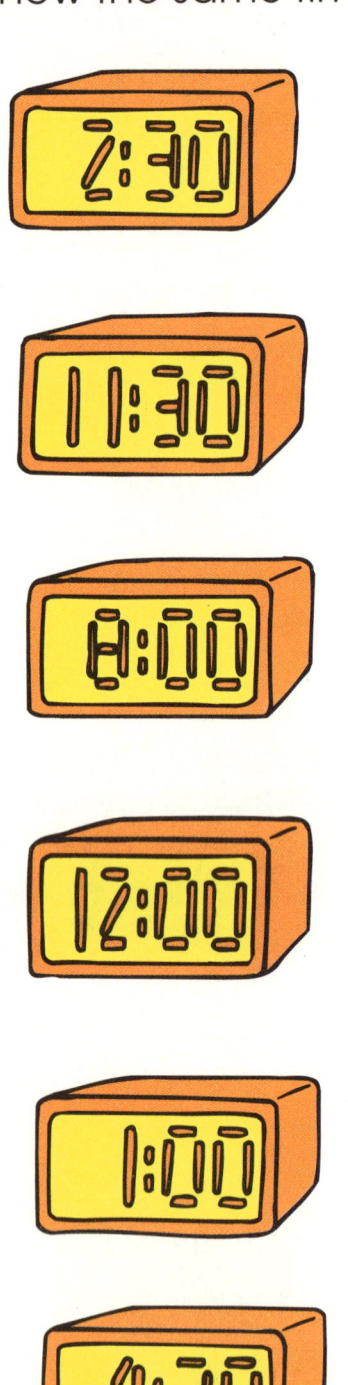

Basic Skills Helpers: Grade 2   68   ©2006 School Specialty Publishing

Name _____

2-Digit Addition

Directions: Study the example. Follow the steps to add.

Example: 33
+41

Step 1: Add the ones.

tens	ones
3	3
+4	1
	4

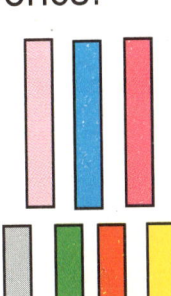

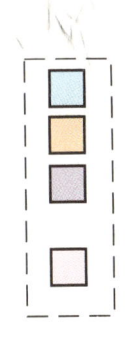

Step 2: Add the tens.

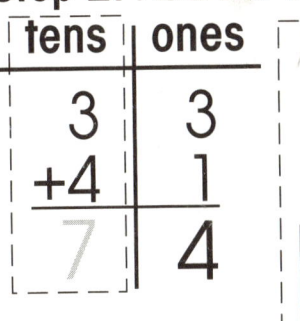

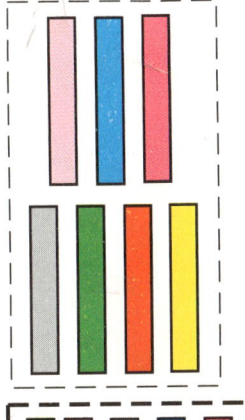

tens	ones
3	3
+4	1
7	4

tens	ones
4	2
+2	4
6	6

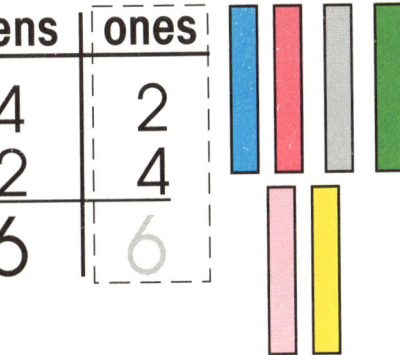

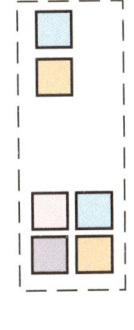

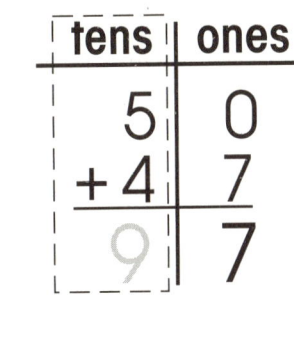

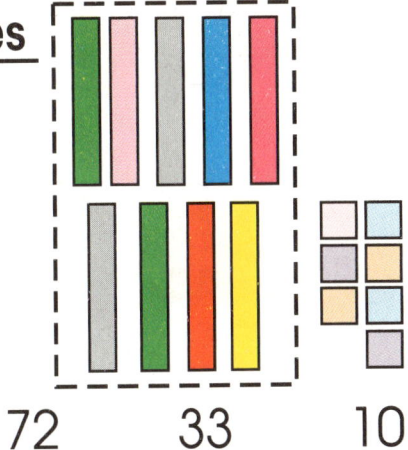

tens	ones
5	0
+4	7
9	7

24   15   38   11   37   72   33   10
+62 +23 +61 +26 +42 +11 +51 +30

25   62   32   25   82   91   16   55
+42 +14 +44 +13 + 6 + 5 +71 + 3

Name _____

Place Value: Ones, Tens

The place value of a digit or numeral is shown by where it is in the number. For example, in the number **23**, **2** has the place value of **tens**, and **3** is **ones**.

Directions: Add the tens and ones and write your answers in the blanks.

Example:

3 tens   +   3 ones   =   _33_

                 tens ones   tens ones

7 tens + 5 ones = _____   4 tens + 0 ones = _____
2 tens + 3 ones = _____   8 tens + 1 one = _____
5 tens + 2 ones = _____   1 ten + 1 one = _____
5 tens + 4 ones = _____   6 tens + 3 ones = _____
9 tens + 5 ones = _____

Directions: Draw a line to the correct number.

         6 tens + 7 ones   73
         4 tens + 2 ones   67
         8 tens + 0 ones   51
         7 tens + 3 ones   80
         5 tens + 1 one   42

Name _____

Money: Penny, Nickel, Dime

Directions: Draw a line from the toy to the amount of money it costs.

Name _____

Money: Quarter

A quarter is worth 25¢.

Directions: Count the coins and write the amounts.

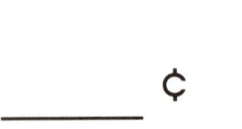

_____ ¢   _____ ¢

_____ ¢   _____ ¢

_____ ¢   _____ ¢

_____ ¢   _____ ¢

Answer Key

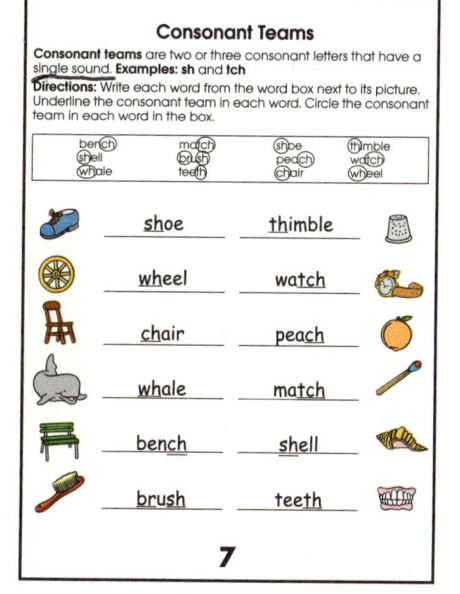

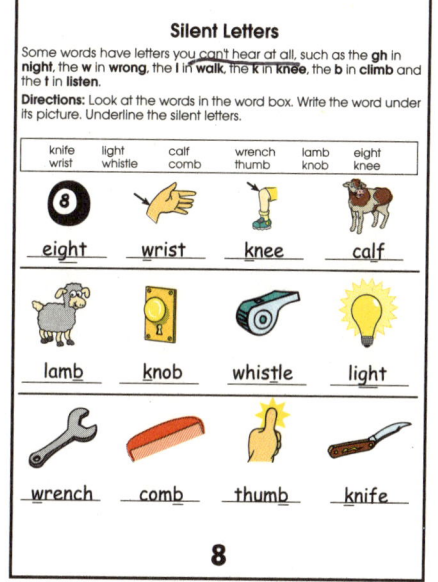

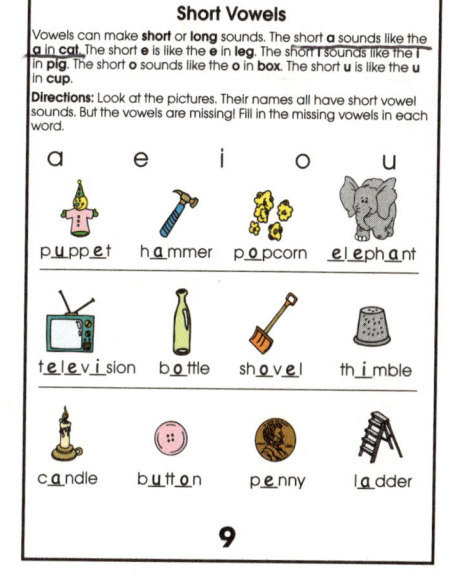

Consonant Blends

Consonant blends are two or three consonant letters in a word whose sounds combine, or blend. **Examples:** br, fr, gr, pr, tr
Directions: Look at each picture. Say its name. Write the blend you hear at the beginning of each word.

tr	fr	br
pr	tr	gr
fr	gr	br
tr	pr	tr

4

Blends: fl, br, pl, sk, sn

Blends are two consonants put together to form a single sound.
Directions: Look at the pictures and say their names. Write the letters for the beginning sound in each word.

br	sk
fl	br
fl	sn
br	pl
sn	fl
sk	pl

5

Blends: bl, sl, cr, cl

Directions: Look at the pictures and say their names. Write the letters for the beginning sound in each word.

cl own	bl anket	cr ayon
cl ock	sl ide	cl oud
sl ed	cr ab	cr ocodile

6

Consonant Teams

Consonant teams are two or three consonant letters that have a single sound. **Examples:** sh and tch
Directions: Write each word from the word box next to its picture. Underline the consonant team in each word. Circle the consonant team in each word in the box.

ben(ch) ma(tch) (sh)oe (th)imble
(sh)ell bru(sh) pea(ch) wa(tch)
(wh)ale tee(th) (ch)air (wh)eel

shoe	thimble
wheel	watch
chair	peach
whale	match
bench	shell
brush	teeth

7

Silent Letters

Some words have letters you can't hear at all, such as the **gh** in **night**, the **w** in **wrong**, the **l** in **walk**, the **k** in **knee**, the **b** in **climb** and the **t** in **listen**.
Directions: Look at the words in the word box. Write the word under its picture. Underline the silent letters.

knife light calf wrench lamb eight
wrist whistle comb thumb knob knee

eight	wrist	knee	calf
lamb	knob	whistle	light
wrench	comb	thumb	knife

8

Short Vowels

Vowels can make **short** or long sounds. The short **a** sounds like the **a** in **cat**. The short **e** is like the **e** in **leg**. The short **i** sounds like the **i** in **pig**. The short **o** sounds like the **o** in **box**. The short **u** is like the **u** in **cup**.
Directions: Look at the pictures. Their names all have short vowel sounds. But the vowels are missing! Fill in the missing vowels in each word.

a   e   i   o   u

p u ppet	h a mmer	p o pcorn	el e phant
t e lev i sion	b o ttle	sh o vel	th i mble
c a ndle	b u tt o n	p e nny	l a dder

9

©2006 School Specialty Publishing   71   Basic Skills Helpers: Grade 2

Long Vowels

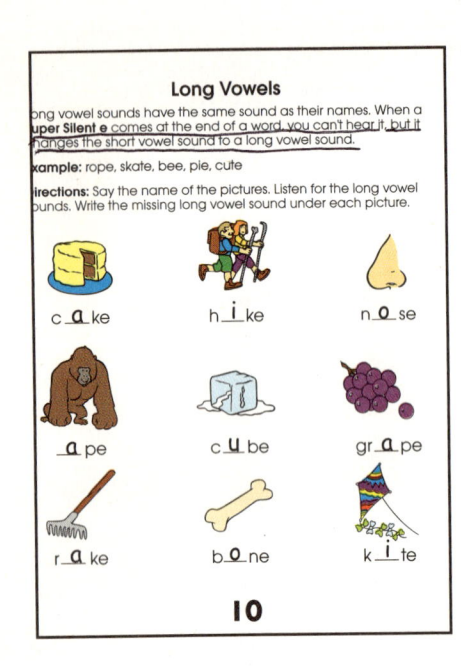

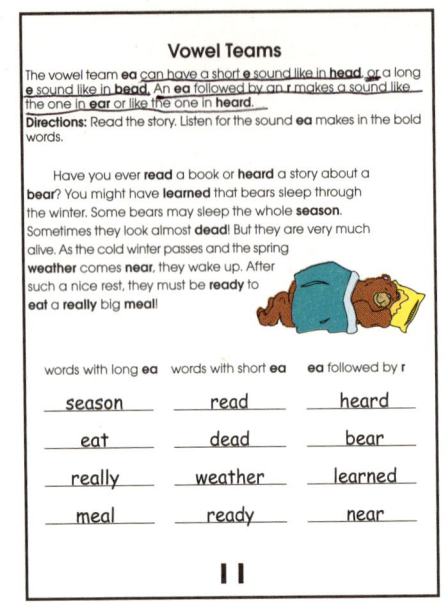

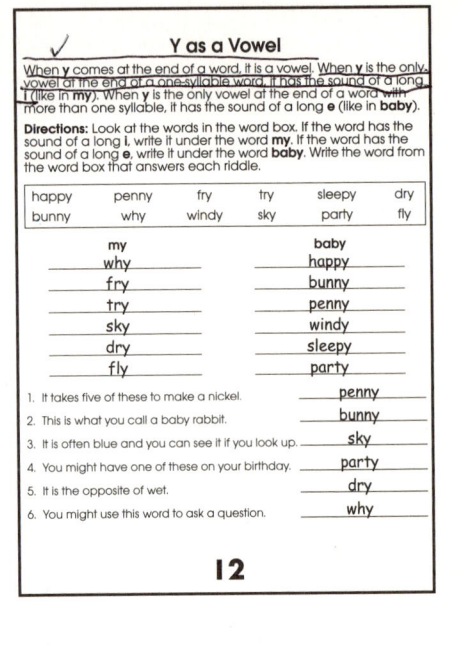

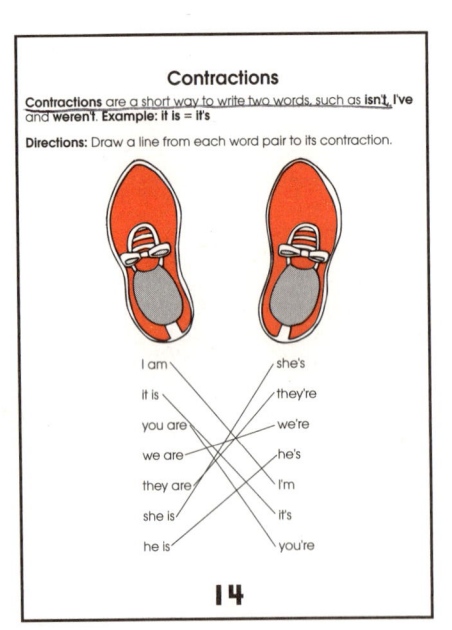

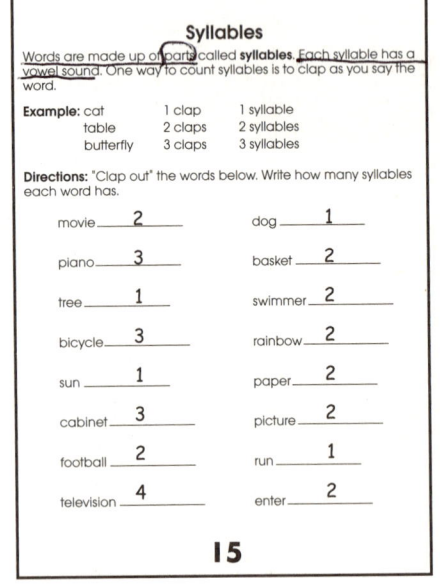

Long vowel sounds have the same sound as their names. When a **Super Silent e** comes at the end of a word, you can't hear it, but it changes the short vowel sound to a long vowel sound.

Example: rope, skate, bee, pie, cute

Directions: Say the name of the pictures. Listen for the long vowel sounds. Write the missing long vowel sound under each picture.

c _a_ ke   h _i_ ke   n _o_ se

_a_ pe   c _u_ be   gr _a_ pe

r _a_ ke   b _o_ ne   k _i_ te

10

Vowel Teams

The vowel team **ea** can have a short **e** sound like in **head**, or a long **e** sound like in **bead**. An **ea** followed by an **r** makes a sound like the one in **ear** or like the one in **heard**.

Directions: Read the story. Listen for the sound **ea** makes in the bold words.

Have you ever **read** a book or **heard** a story about a **bear**? You might have **learned** that bears sleep through the winter. Some bears may sleep the whole **season**. Sometimes they look almost **dead**! But they are very much alive. As the cold winter passes and the spring **weather** comes **near**, they wake up. After such a nice rest, they must be **ready** to **eat** a **really** big **meal**!

words with long ea	words with short ea	ea followed by r
season	read	heard
eat	dead	bear
really	weather	learned
meal	ready	near

11

Y as a Vowel

When **y** comes at the end of a word, it is a vowel. When **y** is the only vowel at the end of a one-syllable word, it has the sound of a long **i** (like in **my**). When **y** is the only vowel at the end of a word with more than one syllable, it has the sound of a long **e** (like in **baby**).

Directions: Look at the words in the word box. If the word has the sound of a long **i**, write it under the word **my**. If the word has the sound of a long **e**, write it under the word **baby**. Write the word from the word box that answers each riddle.

| happy | penny | fry | try | sleepy | dry |
| bunny | why | windy | sky | party | fly |

my	baby
why	happy
fry	bunny
try	penny
sky	windy
dry	sleepy
fly	party

1. It takes five of these to make a nickel.   penny
2. This is what you call a baby rabbit.   bunny
3. It is often blue and you can see if you look up.   sky
4. You might have one of these on your birthday.   party
5. It is the opposite of wet.   dry
6. You might use this word to ask a question.   why

12

Compound Words

Compound words are formed by putting together two smaller words.

Directions: Help the cook brew her stew. Mix words from the first column with words from the second column to make new words. Write your new words on the lines at the bottom.

grand	brows
snow	light
eye	stairs
down	string
rose	book
shoe	mother
note	ball
moon	bud

1. grandmother   5. rosebud
2. snowball   6. shoestring
3. eyebrows   7. notebook
4. downstairs   8. moonlight

13

Contractions

Contractions are a short way to write two words, such as **isn't**, **I've**, and **weren't**. Example: it is = it's

Directions: Draw a line from each word pair to its contraction.

I am — she's
it is — they're
you are — we're
we are — he's
they are — I'm
she is — it's
he is — you're

14

Syllables

Words are made up of parts called **syllables**. Each syllable has a vowel sound. One way to count syllables is to clap as you say the word.

Example:
cat   1 clap   1 syllable
table   2 claps   2 syllables
butterfly   3 claps   3 syllables

Directions: "Clap out" the words below. Write how many syllables each word has.

movie 2   dog 1
piano 3   basket 2
tree 1   swimmer 2
bicycle 3   rainbow 2
sun 1   paper 2
cabinet 3   picture 2
football 2   run 1
television 4   enter 2

15

Syllables

Dividing a word into syllables can help you read a new word. You also might divide syllables when you are writing if you run out of space on a line.
Many words contain two consonants that are next to each other. A word can usually be divided between the consonants.

Directions: Divide each word into two syllables. The first one is done for you.

kitten	kit	ten
lumber	lum	ber
batter	bat	ter
winter	win	ter
funny	fun	ny
harder	hard	er
dirty	dir	ty
sister	sis	ter
little	lit	tle
dinner	din	ner

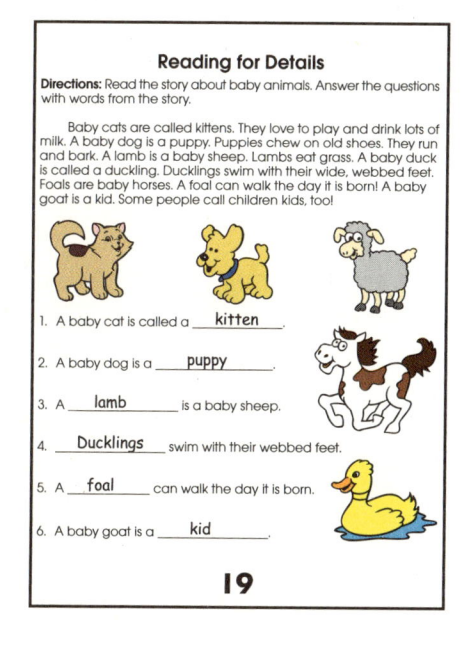

16

Suffixes

A **suffix** is a syllable that is added at the end of a word to change its meaning.
Directions: Add the suffixes to the root words to make new words. Use your new words to complete the sentences.

help + ful = helpful
care + less = careless
build + er = builder
talk + ed = talked
love + ly = lovely
loud + er = louder

1. My mother _talked_ to my teacher about my homework.
2. The radio was _louder_ than the television.
3. Sally is always _helpful_ to her mother.
4. A _builder_ put a new garage on our house.
5. The flowers are _lovely_.
6. It is _careless_ to cross the street without looking both ways.

17

Prefixes

Directions: Change the meaning of the sentences by adding the prefixes to the **bold** words.

The boy was **lucky** because he guessed the answer **correctly**.
The boy was (un) _unlucky_ because he guessed the answer (in) _incorrectly_.

When Mary **behaved**, she felt **happy**.
When Mary (mis) _misbehaved_, she felt (un) _unhappy_.

Mike wore his jacket **buttoned** because the dance was **formal**.
Mike wore his jacket (un) _unbuttoned_ because the dance was (in) _informal_.

Tim **understood** because he was **familiar** with the book.
Tim (mis) _misunderstood_ because he was (un) _unfamiliar_ with the book.

18

Reading for Details

Directions: Read the story about baby animals. Answer the questions with words from the story.

Baby cats are called kittens. They love to play and drink lots of milk. A baby dog is a puppy. Puppies chew on old shoes. They run and bark. A lamb is a baby sheep. Lambs eat grass. A baby duck is called a duckling. Ducklings swim with their wide, webbed feet. Foals are baby horses. A foal can walk the day it is born! A baby goat is a kid. Some people call children kids, too!

1. A baby cat is called a _kitten_.
2. A baby dog is a _puppy_.
3. A _lamb_ is a baby sheep.
4. _Ducklings_ swim with their webbed feet.
5. A _foal_ can walk the day it is born.
6. A baby goat is a _kid_.

19

Reading for Details

Directions: Read the story about bike safety. Answer the questions below the story.

Mike has a red bike. He likes his bike. Mike wears a helmet. Mike wears knee pads and elbow pads. They keep him safe. Mike stops at signs. Mike looks both ways. Mike is safe on his bike.

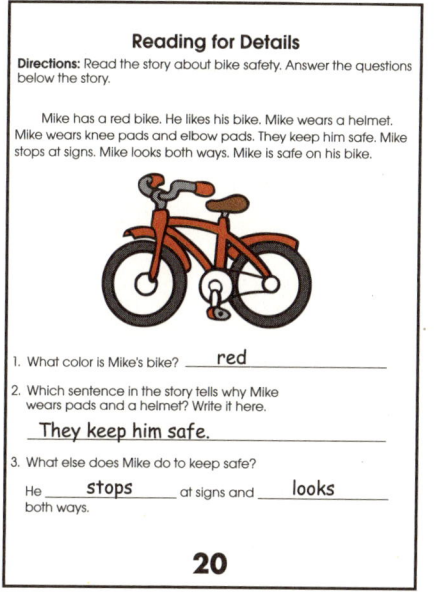

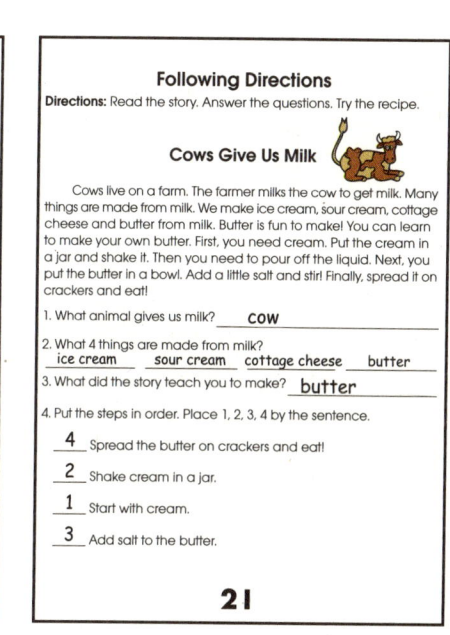

1. What color is Mike's bike? _red_
2. Which sentence in the story tells why Mike wears pads and a helmet? Write it here.
   They keep him safe.
3. What else does Mike do to keep safe?
   He _stops_ at signs and _looks_ both ways.

20

Following Directions

Directions: Read the story. Answer the questions. Try the recipe.

Cows Give Us Milk

Cows live on a farm. The farmer milks the cow to get milk. Many things are made from milk. We make ice cream, sour cream, cottage cheese and butter from milk. Butter is fun to make! You can learn to make your own butter. First, you need cream. Put the cream in a jar and shake it. Then you need to pour off the liquid. Next, you put the butter in a bowl. Add a little salt and stir! Finally, spread it on crackers and eat!

1. What animal gives us milk? _cow_
2. What 4 things are made from milk?
   ice cream _sour cream_ _cottage cheese_ _butter_
3. What did the story teach you to make? _butter_
4. Put the steps in order. Place 1, 2, 3, 4 by the sentence.
   _4_ Spread the butter on crackers and eat!
   _2_ Shake cream in a jar.
   _1_ Start with cream.
   _3_ Add salt to the butter.

21

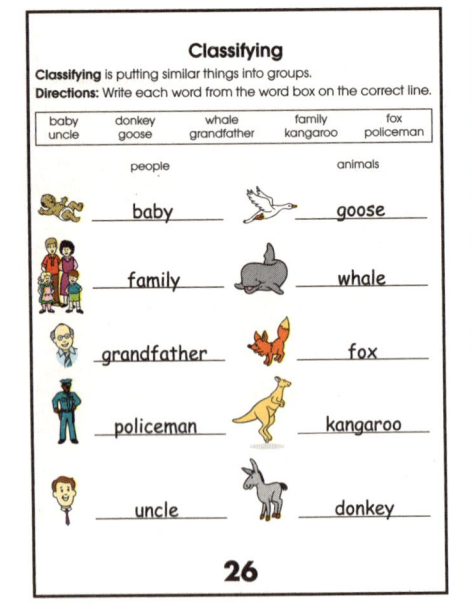

Sequencing: Yo-Yo Trick
Directions: Read about the yo-yo trick.

Wind up the yo-yo string. Hold the yo-yo in your hand. Now, hold your palm up. Throw the yo-yo downward on the string. Hold your palm down. Now, swing the yo-yo forward. Make it "walk." This yo-yo trick is called "walk the dog."

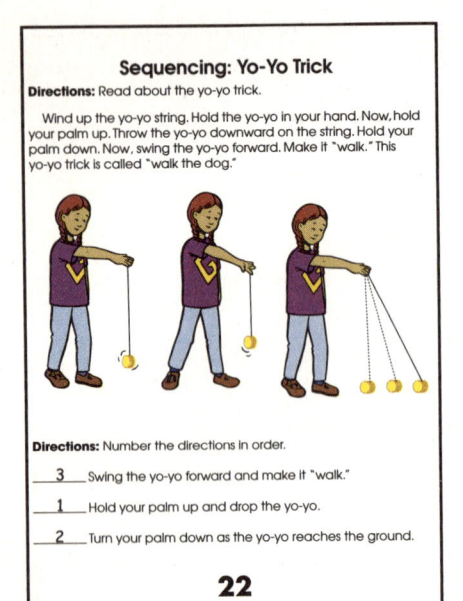

Directions: Number the directions in order.

_3_ Swing the yo-yo forward and make it "walk."
_1_ Hold your palm up and drop the yo-yo.
_2_ Turn your palm down as the yo-yo reaches the ground.

22

Sequencing: A Visit to the Zoo
Directions: Read the story. Then follow the instructions.

One Saturday morning in May, Gloria and Anna went to the zoo. First, they bought tickets to get into the zoo. Second, they visited the Gorilla Garden and had fun watching the gorillas stare at them. Then they went to Tiger Town and watched the tigers as they slept in the sunshine. Fourth, they went to Hippo Haven and laughed at the hippos cooling off in their pool. Next, they visited Snake Station and learned about poisonous and nonpoisonous snakes. It was noon, and they were hungry, so they ate lunch at the Parrot Patio.

Write **first**, **second**, **third**, **fourth**, **fifth** and **sixth** to put the events in order.

Fourth They went to Hippo Haven.
First Gloria and Anna bought zoo tickets.
Third They watched the tigers sleep.
Sixth They ate lunch at Parrot Patio.
Second The gorillas stared at them.
Fifth They learned about poisonous and nonpoisonous snakes.

23

Same/Different: Cats and Tigers
Directions: Read about cats and tigers. Then complete the Venn diagram, telling how they are the same and different.

Tigers are a kind of cat. Pet cats and tigers both have fur. Pet cats are small and tame. Tigers are large and wild.

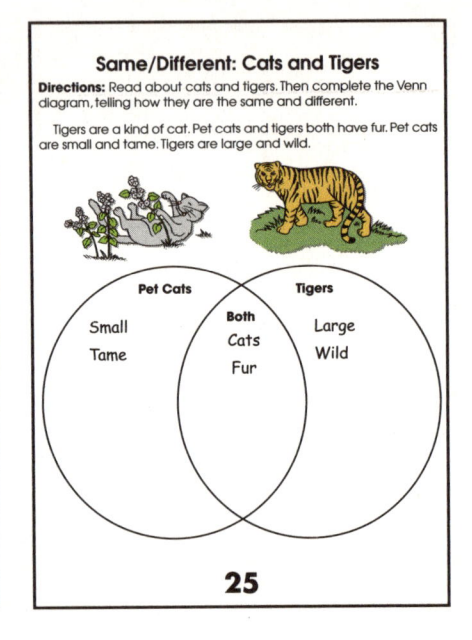

Pet Cats: Small, Tame
Both: Cats, Fur
Tigers: Large, Wild

25

Classifying
Classifying is putting similar things into groups.
Directions: Write each word from the word box on the correct line.

| baby | donkey | whale | family | fox |
| uncle | goose | grandfather | kangaroo | policeman |

people
baby
family
grandfather
policeman
uncle

animals
goose
whale
fox
kangaroo
donkey

26

Classifying: Words
Dapper Dog is going camping.
Directions: Draw an **X** on the word in each row that does not belong in that group.

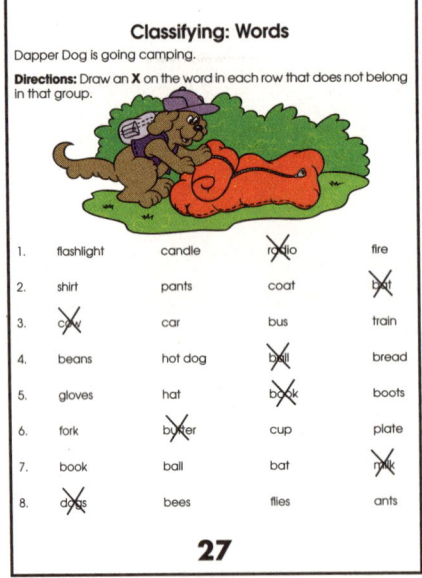

1. flashlight   candle   ~~radio~~   fire
2. shirt   pants   coat   ~~hat~~
3. ~~cow~~   car   bus   train
4. beans   hot dog   ~~ball~~   bread
5. gloves   hat   ~~book~~   boots
6. fork   ~~butter~~   cup   plate
7. book   ball   bat   ~~milk~~
8. ~~dogs~~   bees   flies   ants

27

Comprehension: Types of Tops
The **main idea** is the most important point or idea in a story.
Directions: Read about tops. Then answer the questions.

Tops come in all sizes. Some tops are made of wood. Some tops are made of tin. All tops do the same thing. They spin! Do you have a top?

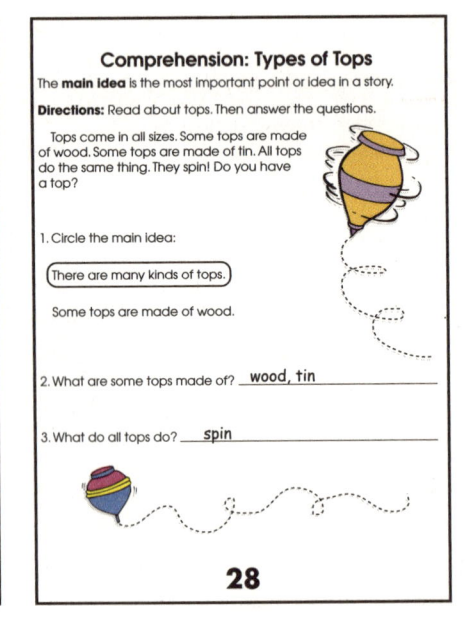

1. Circle the main idea:
   (There are many kinds of tops.)
   Some tops are made of wood.

2. What are some tops made of? _wood, tin_

3. What do all tops do? _spin_

28

Comprehension: Singing Whales

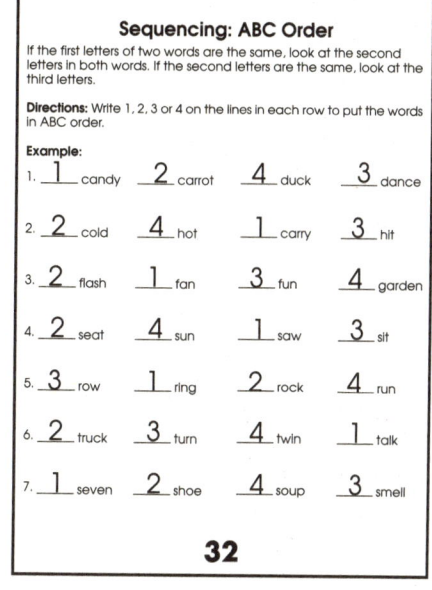

Directions: Read about singing whales. Then follow the instructions.

Some whales can sing! We cannot understand the words. But we can hear the tune of the humpback whale. Each season, humpback whales sing a different song.

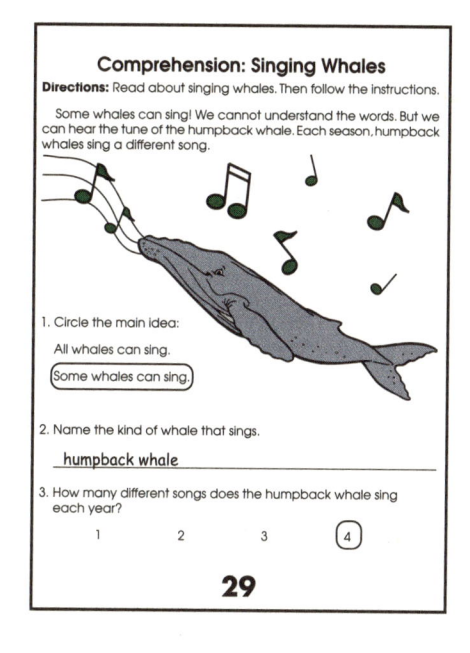

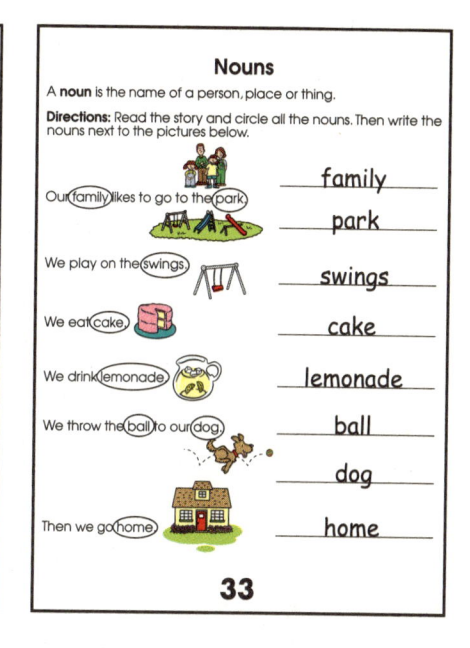

1. Circle the main idea:
   All whales can sing.
   (Some whales can sing.)

2. Name the kind of whale that sings.
   humpback whale

3. How many different songs does the humpback whale sing each year?
   1   2   3   (4)

29

Sequencing: ABC Order

If the first letters of two words are the same, look at the second letters in both words. If the second letters are the same, look at the third letters.

Directions: Write 1, 2, 3 or 4 on the lines in each row to put the words in ABC order.

Example:
1. _1_ candy   _2_ carrot   _4_ duck   _3_ dance
2. _2_ cold   _4_ hot   _1_ carry   _3_ hit
3. _2_ flash   _1_ fan   _3_ fun   _4_ garden
4. _2_ seat   _4_ sun   _1_ saw   _3_ sit
5. _3_ row   _1_ ring   _2_ rock   _4_ run
6. _2_ truck   _3_ turn   _4_ twin   _1_ talk
7. _1_ seven   _2_ shoe   _4_ soup   _3_ smell

32

Nouns

A **noun** is the name of a person, place or thing.

Directions: Read the story and circle all the nouns. Then write the nouns next to the pictures below.

Our (family) likes to go to the (park).   family
                                          park
We play on the (swings).   swings
We eat (cake).   cake
We drink (lemonade).   lemonade
We throw the (ball) to our (dog).   ball
                                          dog
Then we go (home).   home

33

Subjects

The **subject** of a sentence is the person, place or thing the sentence is about.

Directions: Underline the subject in each sentence.

Example: Mom read a book.
(Think: Who is the sentence about? Mom)

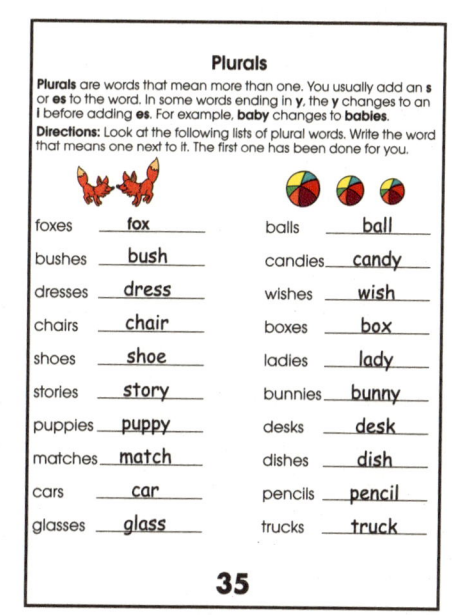

1. The <u>bird</u> flew away.
2. The <u>kite</u> was high in the air.
3. The <u>children</u> played a game.
4. The <u>books</u> fell down.
5. The <u>monkey</u> climbed a tree.

34

Plurals

Plurals are words that mean more than one. You usually add an **s** or **es** to the word. In some words ending in **y**, the **y** changes to an **i** before adding **es**. For example, **baby** changes to **babies**.

Directions: Look at the following lists of plural words. Write the word that means one next to it. The first one has been done for you.

foxes	fox	balls	ball
bushes	bush	candies	candy
dresses	dress	wishes	wish
chairs	chair	boxes	box
shoes	shoe	ladies	lady
stories	story	bunnies	bunny
puppies	puppy	desks	desk
matches	match	dishes	dish
cars	car	pencils	pencil
glasses	glass	trucks	truck

35

Verbs

A **verb** is the action word in a sentence. Verbs tell what something does or that something exists.

Example: **Run**, **sleep** and **jump** are verbs.

Directions: Circle the verbs in the sentences below.

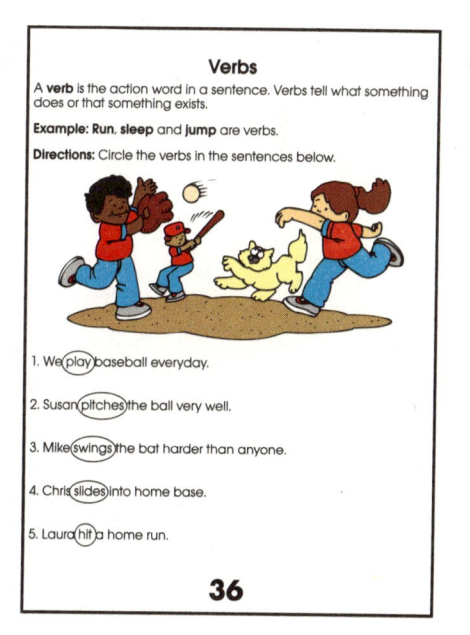

1. We (play) baseball everyday.
2. Susan (pitches) the ball very well.
3. Mike (swings) the bat harder than anyone.
4. Chris (slides) into home base.
5. Laura (hit) a home run.

36

©2006 School Specialty Publishing   75   Basic Skills Helpers: Grade 2

Predicates

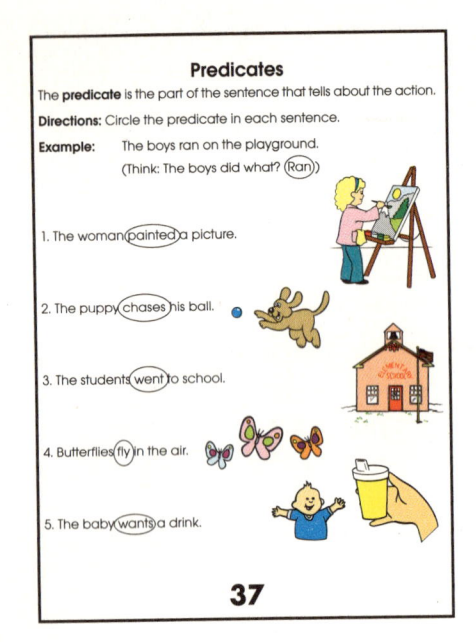

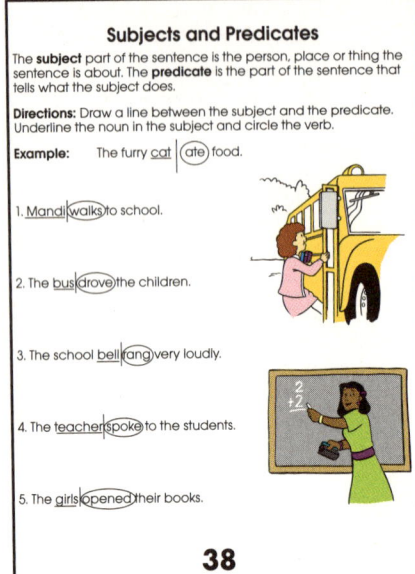

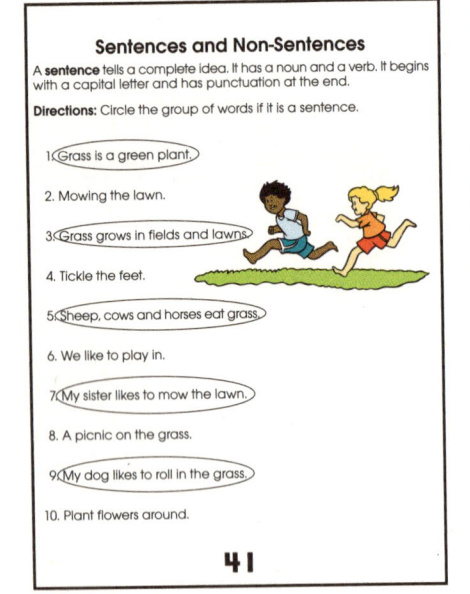

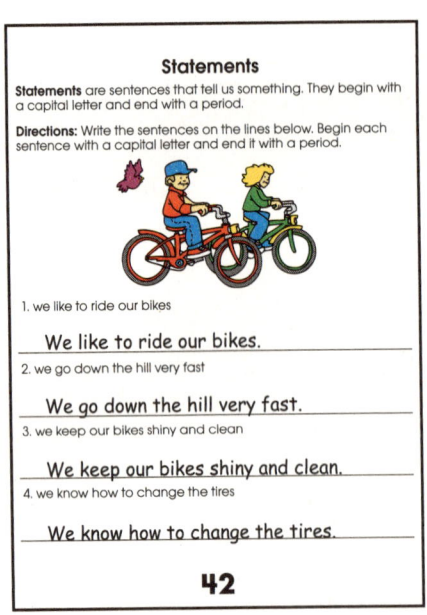

The **predicate** is the part of the sentence that tells about the action.

Directions: Circle the predicate in each sentence.

Example: The boys ran on the playground.
(Think: The boys did what? (Ran))

1. The woman (painted) a picture.
2. The puppy (chases) his ball.
3. The students (went) to school.
4. Butterflies (fly) in the air.
5. The baby (wants) a drink.

37

Subjects and Predicates

The **subject** part of the sentence is the person, place or thing the sentence is about. The **predicate** is the part of the sentence that tells what the subject does.

Directions: Draw a line between the subject and the predicate. Underline the noun in the subject and circle the verb.

Example: The furry <u>cat</u> | (ate) food.

1. <u>Mandi</u> (walks) to school.
2. The <u>bus</u> (drove) the children.
3. The school <u>bell</u> (rang) very loudly.
4. The <u>teacher</u> (spoke) to the students.
5. The <u>girls</u> (opened) their books.

38

Adjectives

Adjectives are words that tell more about a person, place or thing.

Examples: cold, fuzzy, dark

Directions: Circle the adjectives in the sentences.

1. The (juicy) apple is on the plate.
2. The (furry) dog is eating a bone.
3. It was a (sunny) day.
4. The kitten drinks (warm) milk.
5. The baby has a (loud) cry.

39

Sentences and Non-Sentences

A **sentence** tells a complete idea. It has a noun and a verb. It begins with a capital letter and has punctuation at the end.

Directions: Circle the group of words if it is a sentence.

1. (Grass is a green plant.)
2. Mowing the lawn.
3. (Grass grows in fields and lawns.)
4. Tickle the feet.
5. (Sheep, cows and horses eat grass.)
6. We like to play in.
7. (My sister likes to mow the lawn.)
8. A picnic on the grass.
9. (My dog likes to roll in the grass.)
10. Plant flowers around.

41

Statements

Statements are sentences that tell us something. They begin with a capital letter and end with a period.

Directions: Write the sentences on the lines below. Begin each sentence with a capital letter and end it with a period.

1. we like to ride our bikes
   We like to ride our bikes.
2. we go down the hill very fast
   We go down the hill very fast.
3. we keep our bikes shiny and clean
   We keep our bikes shiny and clean.
4. we know how to change the tires
   We know how to change the tires.

42

Surprising Sentences

Surprising sentences tell a strong feeling and end with an exclamation point. A surprising sentence may be only one or two words showing fear, surprise or pain. **Example: Oh, no!**

Directions: Put a period at the end of the sentences that tell something. Put an exclamation point at the end of the sentences that tell a strong feeling. Put a question mark at the end of the sentences that ask a question.

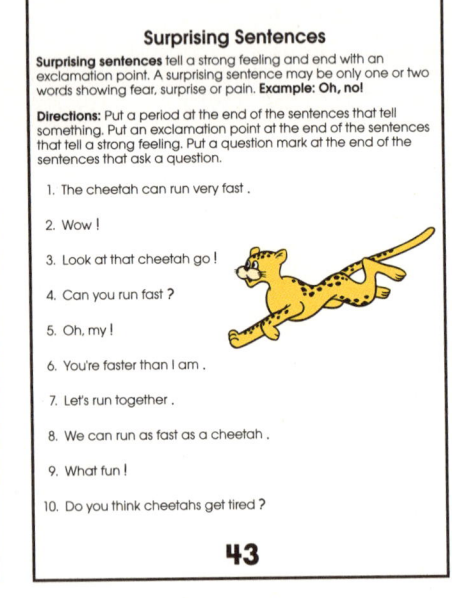

1. The cheetah can run very fast .
2. Wow !
3. Look at that cheetah go !
4. Can you run fast ?
5. Oh, my !
6. You're faster than I am .
7. Let's run together .
8. We can run as fast as a cheetah .
9. What fun !
10. Do you think cheetahs get tired ?

43

Basic Skills Helpers: Grade 2   76   ©2006 School Specialty Publishing

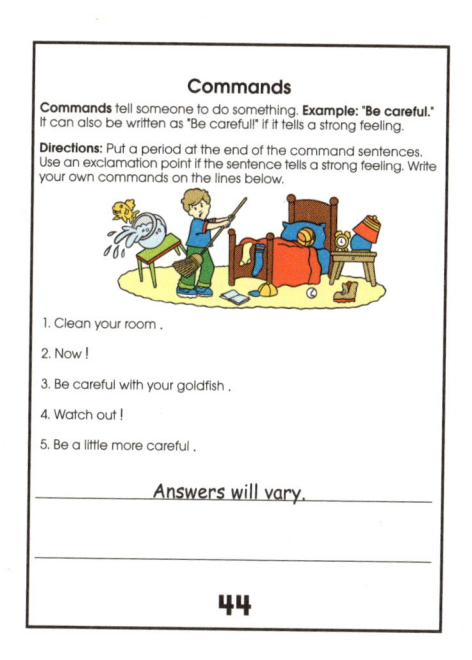

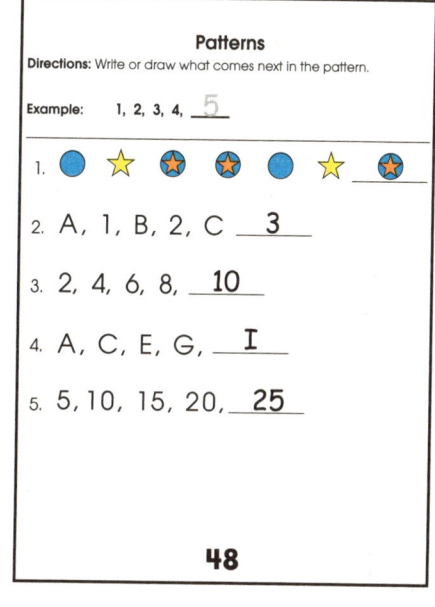

Commands

Commands tell someone to do something. **Example:** "Be careful."
It can also be written as "Be careful!" if it tells a strong feeling.

Directions: Put a period at the end of the command sentences.
Use an exclamation point if the sentence tells a strong feeling. Write
your own commands on the lines below.

1. Clean your room .
2. Now !
3. Be careful with your goldfish .
4. Watch out !
5. Be a little more careful .

Answers will vary.

44

Questions

Questions are sentences that ask something. They begin with a
capital letter and end with a question mark.

Directions: Write the questions on the lines below. Begin each
sentence with a capital letter and end it with a question mark.

1. will you be my friend
   Will you be my friend?
2. what is your name
   What is your name?
3. are you eight years old
   Are you eight years old?
4. do you like rainbows
   Do you like rainbows?

45

Counting

Directions: Write the numbers that are:

next in order	one less	one greater
22, 23, _24_, _25_	_15_, 16	6, _7_
674, _675_, _676_	_246_, 247	125, _126_
227, _228_, _229_	_549_, 550	499, _500_
199, _200_, _201_	_332_, 333	750, _751_
329, _330_, _331_	_861_, 862	933, _934_

Directions: Write the missing numbers.

13, 14, 15, 16, 17, 18

163, 164, 165, 166, 167, 168

821, 822, 823, 824, 825, 826

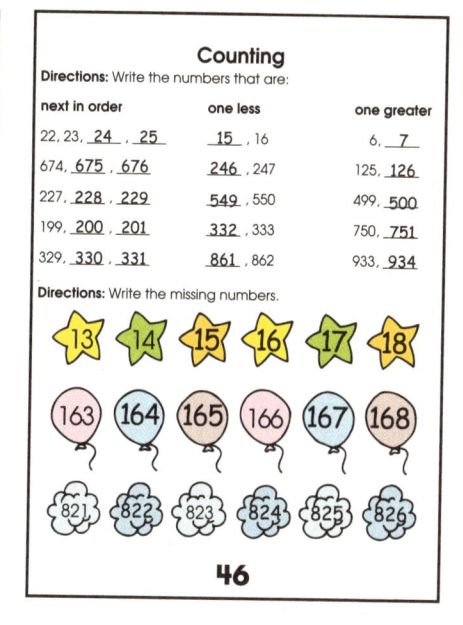

46

Counting: 2's, 5's, 10's

Directions: Write the missing numbers.

Count by 2's:
2, 4, 6, 8, 10, 12, 14, 16, 18, 20

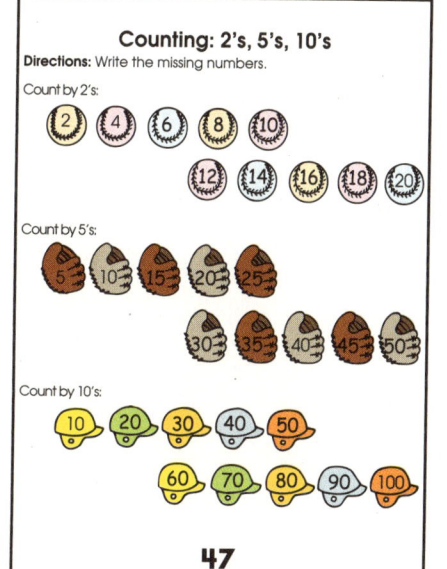

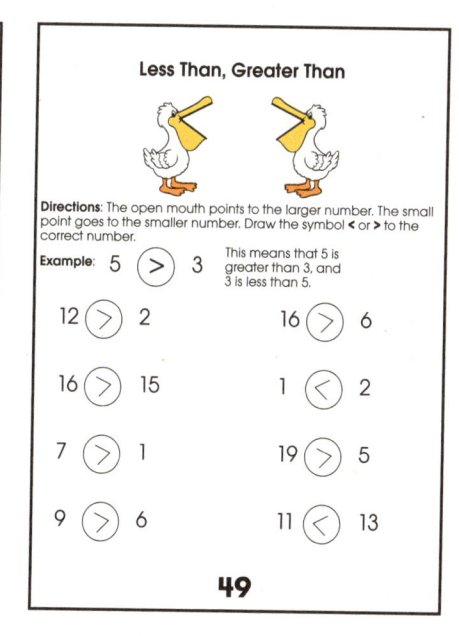

Count by 5's:
5, 10, 15, 20, 25, 30, 35, 40, 45, 50

Count by 10's:
10, 20, 30, 40, 50, 60, 70, 80, 90, 100

47

Patterns

Directions: Write or draw what comes next in the pattern.

Example: 1, 2, 3, 4, _5_

1. ● ★ ● ● ● ★ _★_
2. A, 1, B, 2, C _3_
3. 2, 4, 6, 8, _10_
4. A, C, E, G, _I_
5. 5, 10, 15, 20, _25_

48

Less Than, Greater Than

Directions: The open mouth points to the larger number. The small point goes to the smaller number. Draw the symbol < or > to the correct number.

Example: 5 > 3   This means that 5 is greater than 3, and 3 is less than 5.

12 > 2   16 > 6
16 > 15   1 < 2
7 > 1   19 > 5
9 > 6   11 < 13

49

Ordinal Numbers
Directions: Follow the instructions.

Draw glasses on the second one.
Put a hat on the fourth one.
Color blonde hair on the third one.
Draw a tie on the first one.
Draw ears on the fifth one.
Draw black hair on the seventh one.
Put a bow on the head of the sixth one.

50

Addition
Addition is "putting together" or adding two or more numbers to find the sum.
Directions: Add.
Example:
$\begin{array}{r}2\\+5\\\hline 7\end{array}$

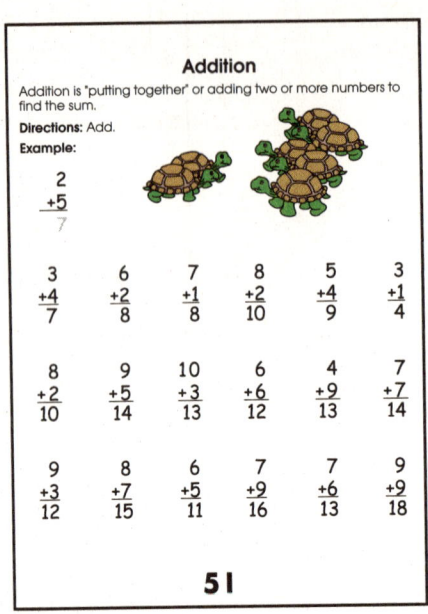

$\begin{array}{r}3\\+4\\\hline 7\end{array}$ $\begin{array}{r}6\\+2\\\hline 8\end{array}$ $\begin{array}{r}7\\+1\\\hline 8\end{array}$ $\begin{array}{r}8\\+2\\\hline 10\end{array}$ $\begin{array}{r}5\\+4\\\hline 9\end{array}$ $\begin{array}{r}3\\+1\\\hline 4\end{array}$

$\begin{array}{r}8\\+2\\\hline 10\end{array}$ $\begin{array}{r}9\\+5\\\hline 14\end{array}$ $\begin{array}{r}10\\+3\\\hline 13\end{array}$ $\begin{array}{r}6\\+6\\\hline 12\end{array}$ $\begin{array}{r}4\\+9\\\hline 13\end{array}$ $\begin{array}{r}7\\+7\\\hline 14\end{array}$

$\begin{array}{r}9\\+3\\\hline 12\end{array}$ $\begin{array}{r}8\\+7\\\hline 15\end{array}$ $\begin{array}{r}6\\+5\\\hline 11\end{array}$ $\begin{array}{r}7\\+9\\\hline 16\end{array}$ $\begin{array}{r}7\\+6\\\hline 13\end{array}$ $\begin{array}{r}9\\+9\\\hline 18\end{array}$

51

Addition: Commutative Property
The commutative property of addition states that even if the order of the numbers is changed in an addition sentence, the sum will stay the same.
Example: $2 + 3 = 5$
$3 + 2 = 5$

Directions: Look at the addition sentences below. Complete the addition sentences by writing the missing numerals.

$5 + 4 = 9$ $3 + 1 = 4$ $2 + 6 = 8$
$4 + \underline{5} = 9$ $1 + \underline{3} = 4$ $6 + \underline{2} = 8$

$6 + 1 = 7$ $4 + 3 = 7$ $1 + 9 = 10$
$1 + \underline{6} = 7$ $3 + \underline{4} = 7$ $9 + \underline{1} = 10$

Now try these:

$6 + 3 = 9$ $10 + 2 = 12$ $8 + 3 = 11$
$\underline{3} + 6 = 9$ $\underline{2} + 10 = 12$ $\underline{3} + 8 = 11$

Look at these sums. Can you think of two number sentences that would show the commutative property of addition?

__ + __ = 7   __ + __ = 11   __ + __ = 9

__ + __ = 7   __ + __ = 11   __ + __ = 9

Answers will vary.

52

Adding 3 or More Numbers
Directions: Add all the numbers to find the sum. Draw pictures to help or break up the problem into two smaller problems.

Example:
$\begin{array}{r}1\\2\\+3\\\hline 6\end{array}$ $\begin{array}{r}+2\\+5\\\hline 7\\+2\\+4\\\hline +6\\\hline 13\end{array}$

$\begin{array}{r}3\\6\\+2\\\hline 11\end{array}$ $\begin{array}{r}8\\5\\+4\\\hline 17\end{array}$ $\begin{array}{r}3\\1\\+5\\\hline 9\end{array}$ $\begin{array}{r}8\\2\\+9\\\hline 19\end{array}$

$\begin{array}{r}2\\8\\+4\\+3\\\hline 17\end{array}$ $\begin{array}{r}3\\6\\5\\+2\\\hline 16\end{array}$ $\begin{array}{r}4\\+5\\+7\\\hline 12\end{array}$ $\begin{array}{r}6\\7\\3\\+1\\\hline 17\end{array}$

53

Subtraction
Subtraction is "taking away" or subtracting one number from another to find the difference.
Directions: Subtract.
Example:
$\begin{array}{r}4\\-3\\\hline 1\end{array}$

$\begin{array}{r}5\\-3\\\hline 2\end{array}$ $\begin{array}{r}6\\-1\\\hline 5\end{array}$ $\begin{array}{r}4\\-3\\\hline 1\end{array}$ $\begin{array}{r}3\\-1\\\hline 2\end{array}$ $\begin{array}{r}2\\-0\\\hline 2\end{array}$ $\begin{array}{r}1\\-1\\\hline 0\end{array}$

$\begin{array}{r}9\\-2\\\hline 7\end{array}$ $\begin{array}{r}7\\-4\\\hline 3\end{array}$ $\begin{array}{r}10\\-5\\\hline 5\end{array}$ $\begin{array}{r}14\\-6\\\hline 8\end{array}$ $\begin{array}{r}15\\-9\\\hline 6\end{array}$ $\begin{array}{r}12\\-3\\\hline 9\end{array}$

$\begin{array}{r}18\\-8\\\hline 10\end{array}$ $\begin{array}{r}13\\-5\\\hline 8\end{array}$ $\begin{array}{r}14\\-7\\\hline 7\end{array}$ $\begin{array}{r}11\\-4\\\hline 7\end{array}$ $\begin{array}{r}17\\-9\\\hline 8\end{array}$ $\begin{array}{r}16\\-8\\\hline 8\end{array}$

54

Place Value: Ones, Tens
The place value of a digit or numeral is shown by where it is in the number. For example, in the number **23**, **2** has the place value of **tens**, and **3** is **ones**.
Directions: Add the tens and ones and write your answers in the blanks.

Example:
3 tens + 3 ones = 33

	tens ones		tens ones
7 tens + 5 ones =	7 5	4 tens + 0 ones =	4 0
2 tens + 3 ones =	2 3	8 tens + 1 one =	8 1
5 tens + 2 ones =	5 2	1 ten + 1 one =	1 1
5 tens + 4 ones =	5 4	6 tens + 3 ones =	6 3
9 tens + 5 ones =	9 5		

Directions: Draw a line to the correct number.

6 tens + 7 ones — 73
4 tens + 2 ones — 67
8 tens + 0 ones — 51
7 tens + 3 ones — 80
5 tens + 1 one — 42

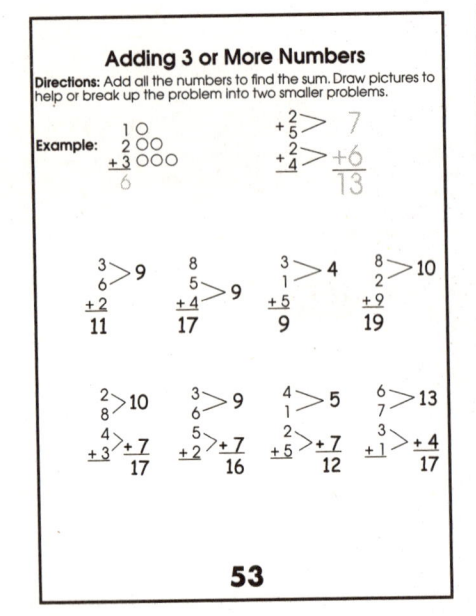

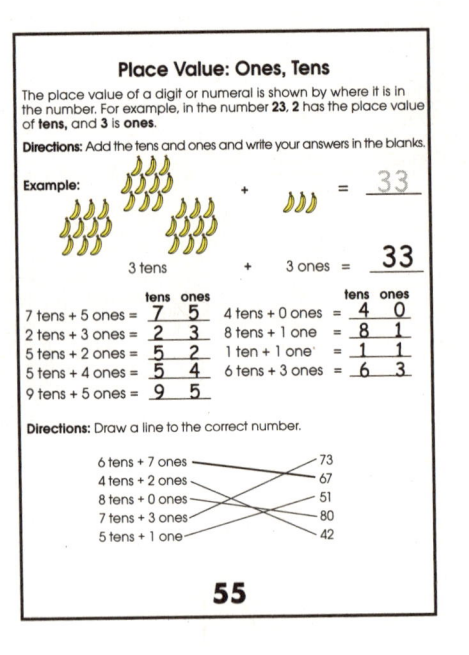

55

2-Digit Addition

Directions: Study the example. Follow the steps to add.

Example: 33
         +41

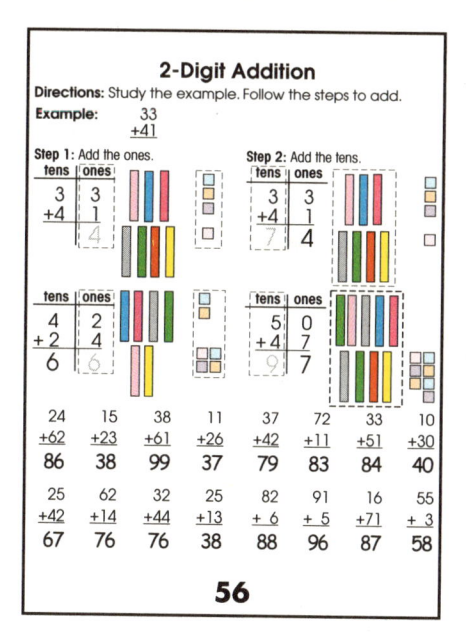

Step 1: Add the ones.
Step 2: Add the tens.

tens	ones
3	3
+4	1
	4

tens	ones
3	3
+4	1
7	4

tens	ones
4	2
+2	4
6	6

tens	ones
5	0
+4	7
9	7

24	15	38	11	37	72	33	10
+62	+23	+61	+26	+42	+11	+51	+30
86	38	99	37	79	83	84	40

25	62	32	25	82	91	16	55
+42	+14	+44	+13	+ 6	+ 5	+71	+ 3
67	76	76	38	88	96	87	58

56

2-Digit Addition: Regrouping

Addition is "putting together" or adding two or more numbers to find the sum. Regrouping is using **ten ones** to form **one ten**, **ten tens** to form **one 100**, **fifteen ones** to form **one ten** and **five ones** and so on.

Directions: Study the examples. Follow the steps to add.

Example: 14
         + 8

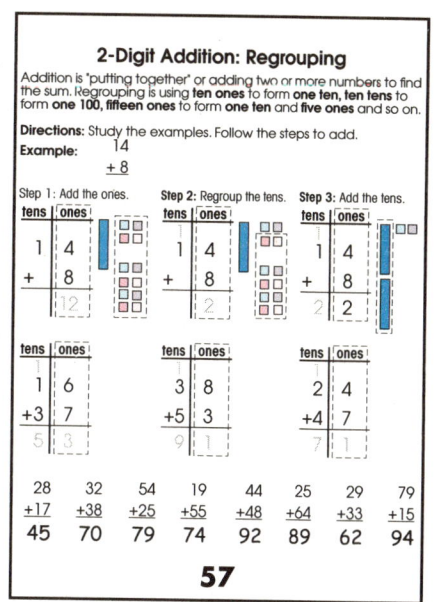

Step 1: Add the ones.   Step 2: Regroup the tens.   Step 3: Add the tens.

tens	ones
1	4
+	8
	12

tens	ones
1	4
+	8
	2

tens	ones
1	4
+	8
2	2

tens	ones
1	6
+3	7
5	3

tens	ones
3	8
+5	3
9	1

tens	ones
2	4
+4	7
7	1

28	32	54	19	44	25	29	79
+17	+38	+25	+55	+48	+64	+33	+15
45	70	79	74	92	89	62	94

57

2-Digit Subtraction

Directions: Study the example. Follow the steps to subtract.

Example: 28
         -14

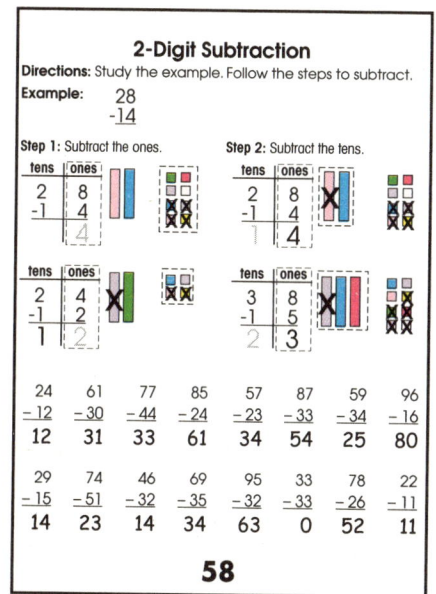

Step 1: Subtract the ones.
Step 2: Subtract the tens.

tens	ones
2	8
-1	4
	4

tens	ones
2	8
-1	4
1	4

tens	ones
2	4
-1	2
	2

tens	ones
3	8
-1	5
2	3

24	61	77	85	57	87	59	96
-12	-30	-44	-24	-23	-33	-34	-16
12	31	33	61	34	54	25	80

29	74	46	69	95	33	78	22
-15	-51	-32	-35	-32	-33	-26	-11
14	23	14	34	63	0	52	11

58

2-Digit Subtraction: Regrouping

Subtraction is "taking away" or subtracting one number from another to find the difference. Regrouping is using **one ten to form ten ones**, **one 100 to form ten tens** and so on.

Directions: Study the examples. Follow the steps to subtract.

Example: 37
         -19

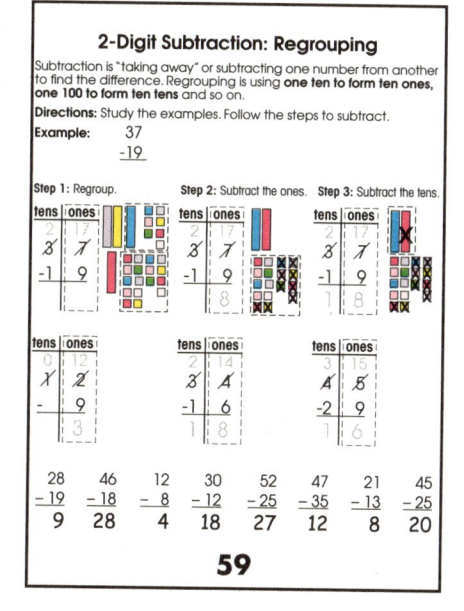

Step 1: Regroup.   Step 2: Subtract the ones.   Step 3: Subtract the tens.

tens	ones
2	17
3	7
-1	9

tens	ones
2	17
3	7
-1	9
	8

tens	ones
2	17
3	7
-1	9
1	8

tens	ones
0	12
1	2
-	9
	3

tens	ones
2	14
3	4
-1	6
1	8

tens	ones
3	15
4	5
-2	9
1	6

28	46	12	30	52	47	21	45
-19	-18	- 8	-12	-25	-35	-13	-25
9	28	4	18	27	12	8	20

59

Graphs

A graph is a drawing that shows information about numbers.

Directions: Count the apples in each row. Color the boxes to show how many apples have bites taken out of them.

Example:

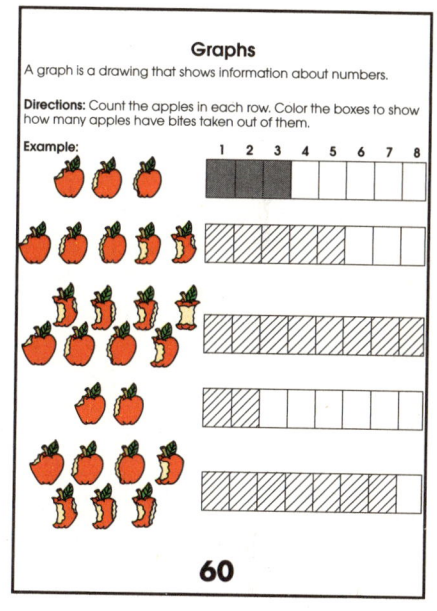

60

Fractions: Half, Third, Fourth

A fraction is a number that names part of a whole, such as $\frac{1}{2}$ or $\frac{1}{3}$.

Directions: Study the examples. Color the correct fraction of each shape.

Examples:

shaded part 1
equal parts 2
$\frac{1}{2}$ (one-half) shaded

shaded part 1
equal parts 3
$\frac{1}{3}$ (one-third) shaded

shaded part 1
equal parts 4
$\frac{1}{4}$ (one-fourth) shaded

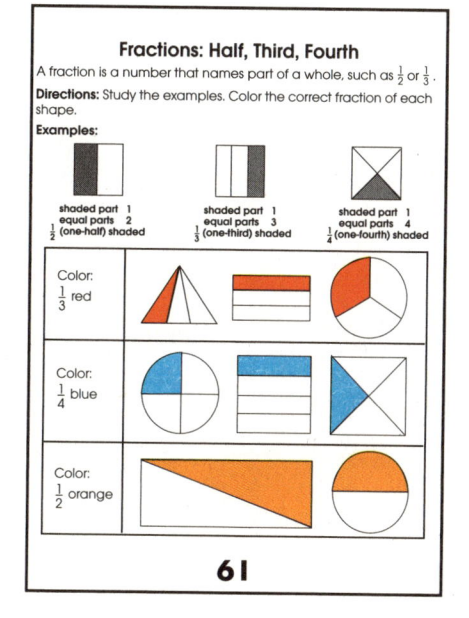

Color: $\frac{1}{3}$ red

Color: $\frac{1}{4}$ blue

Color: $\frac{1}{2}$ orange

61

Fractions: Half, Third, Fourth

Directions: Draw a line from the fraction to the correct shape.

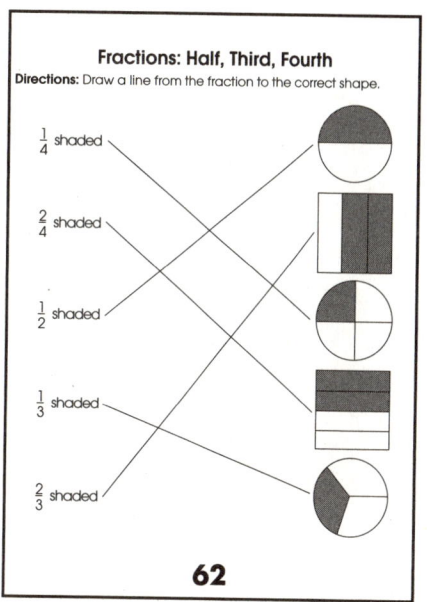

$\frac{1}{4}$ shaded

$\frac{2}{4}$ shaded

$\frac{1}{2}$ shaded

$\frac{1}{3}$ shaded

$\frac{2}{3}$ shaded

62

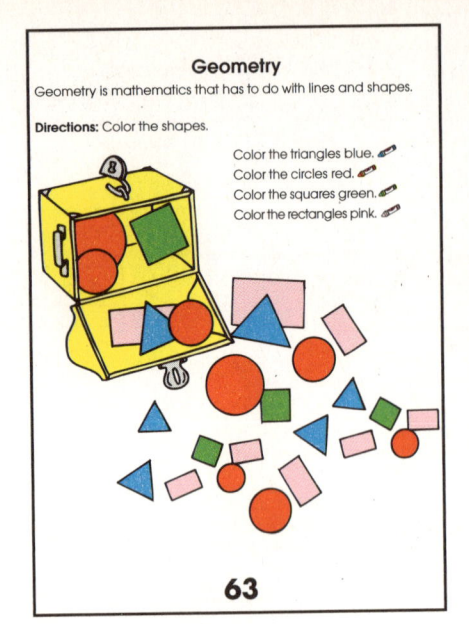

Geometry

Geometry is mathematics that has to do with lines and shapes.

Directions: Color the shapes.

Color the triangles blue.
Color the circles red.
Color the squares green.
Color the rectangles pink.

63

Geometry

Directions: Draw a line from the word to the shape.
Use a red line for circles.   Use a yellow line for rectangles.
Use a blue line for squares. Use a green line for triangles.

Circle   Square   Triangle   Rectangle

64

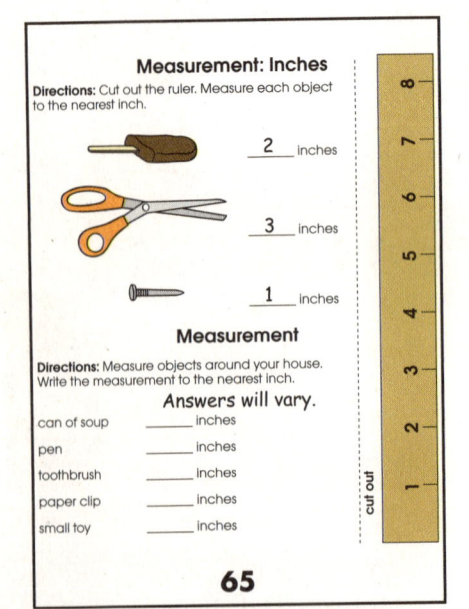

Measurement: Inches

Directions: Cut out the ruler. Measure each object to the nearest inch.

_2_ inches
_3_ inches
_1_ inches

Measurement

Directions: Measure objects around your house. Write the measurement to the nearest inch.

Answers will vary.

can of soup _____ inches
pen _____ inches
toothbrush _____ inches
paper clip _____ inches
small toy _____ inches

65

Time: Hour, Half-Hour

An hour is sixty minutes. The short hand of a clock tells the hour. It is written **0:00**, such as **5:00**. A half-hour is thirty minutes. When the long hand of the clock is pointing to the six, the time is on the half-hour. It is written **:30**, such as **5:30**.

Directions: Study the examples. Tell what time it is on each clock.

Examples:

9:00 — The minute hand is on the 12. The hour hand is on the 9. It is 9 o'clock.

4:30 — The minute hand is on the 6. The hour hand is *between* the 4 and 5. It is 4:30.

2:00   3:30   1:00   5:30   8:00
10:30 12:00 9:30   2:30   3:00

67

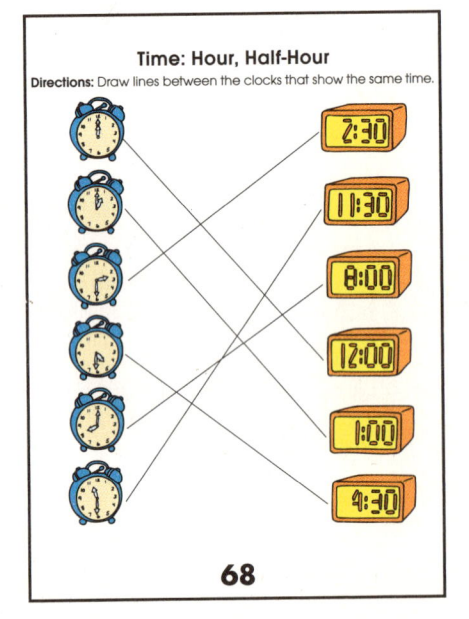

Time: Hour, Half-Hour

Directions: Draw lines between the clocks that show the same time.

2:30
11:30
8:00
12:00
1:00
4:30

68

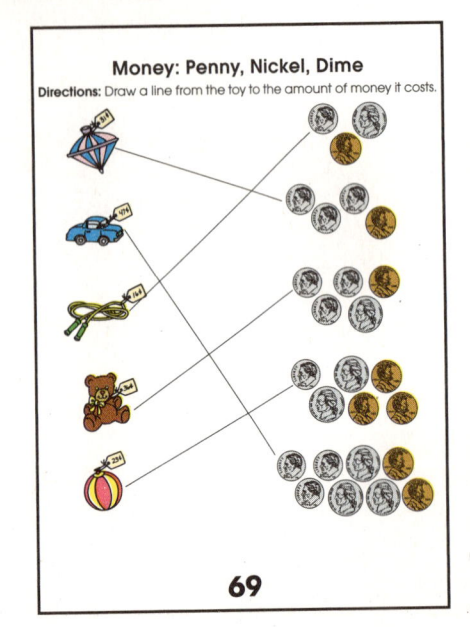

Money: Penny, Nickel, Dime

Directions: Draw a line from the toy to the amount of money it costs.

69

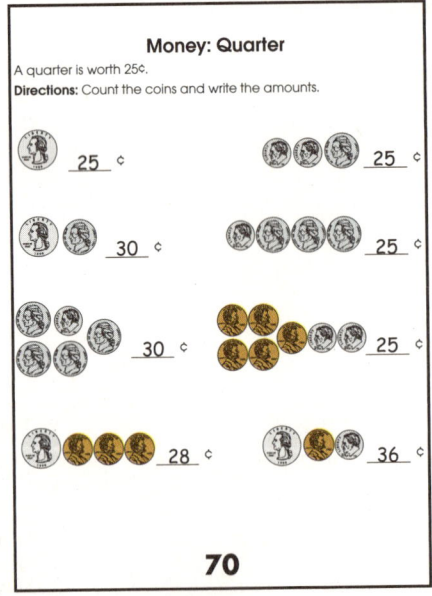

Money: Quarter

A quarter is worth 25¢.

Directions: Count the coins and write the amounts.

_25_ ¢   _25_ ¢
_30_ ¢   _25_ ¢
_30_ ¢   _25_ ¢
_28_ ¢   _36_ ¢

70

Basic Skills Helpers: Grade 2   80   ©2006 School Specialty Publishing